**Draw a Picture of You and Your Mom**

# Mommy & Me

## 100 Daily Devos
### for Moms and Their Little Girls

*The quoted ideas expressed in this book (but not Scripture verses) are not, in all cases, exact quotations, as some have been edited for clarity and brevity. In all cases, the author has attempted to maintain the speaker's original intent. In some cases, quoted material for this book was obtained from secondary sources, primarily print media. While every effort was made to ensure the accuracy of these sources, the accuracy cannot be guaranteed. For additions, deletions, corrections, or clarifications in future editions of this text, please write Freeman-Smith.*

Scripture quotations are taken from:

The Holy Bible, King James Version (KJV)

The Holy Bible, New International Version (NIV) Copyright © 1973, 1978, 1984, by International Bible Society. Used by permission of Zondervan Publishing House. All rights reserved.

The Holy Bible, New King James Version (NKJV) Copyright © 1982 by Thomas Nelson, Inc. Used by permission.

Holy Bible, New Living Translation, (NLT) copyright © 1996. Used by permission of Tyndale House Publishers, Inc., Wheaton, Illinois 60189. All rights reserved.

The Message (MSG)- This edition issued by contractual arrangement with NavPress, a division of The Navigators, U.S.A. Originally published by NavPress in English as THE MESSAGE: The Bible in Contemporary Language copyright 2002-2003 by Eugene Peterson. All rights reserved.

New Century Version®. (NCV) Copyright © 1987, 1988, 1991 by Word Publishing, a division of Thomas Nelson, Inc. All rights reserved. Used by permission.

The New American Standard Bible®, (NASB) Copyright © 1960, 1962, 1963, 1968, 1971, 1972, 1973, 1975, 1977, 1995 by The Lockman Foundation. Used by permission.

International Children's Bible®, New Century Version®. (ICB) Copyright © 1986, 1988, 1999 by Tommy Nelson™, a division of Thomas Nelson, Inc. All rights reserved. Used by permission.

The Holy Bible, The Living Bible (TLB), Copyright © 1971 owned by assignment by Illinois Regional Bank N.A. (as trustee). Used by permission of Tyndale House Publishers, Inc., Wheaton, Illinois 60189. All rights reserved.

The Holman Christian Standard Bible™ (HCSB) Copyright © 1999, 2000, 2001 by Holman Bible Publishers. Used by permission.

Cover Design by Kim Russell / Wahoo Designs
Page Layout by Bart Dawson

ISBN 978-1-60587-360-2

# Mommy & Me

## 100 Daily Devos
### for Moms and Their Little Girls

# A Message to Moms

**P**erhaps your daughter's library is already overflowing with brightly colored children's books. If so, congratulations: you're a thoughtful mother who understands the importance of reading to your child. This little book is an important addition to your child's library. It is intended to be read by Christian moms to their young daughters.

For the next 100 days, try this experiment: read one chapter each night to your daughter, and then spend a few more moments talking about the chapter's meaning. When you do, you will have 100 different opportunities to share God's wisdom with your daughter, and that's a very good thing.

If you have been touched by God's love and His grace, then you know the joy that He has brought into your own life. Now it's your turn to share His message with the girl whom He has entrusted to your care. Happy reading! And may God richly bless you and your family now and forever.

# Jesus Gives Life

*Then Jesus said, "I am the bread that gives life. Whoever comes to me will never be hungry, and whoever believes in me will never be thirsty."*

**John 6:35 NCV**

Who's the best friend any girl has ever had? And who's the best friend the whole wide world has ever had? Jesus, of course! When you invite Him into your heart, Jesus will be your friend, too . . . your friend forever.

Jesus has offered to share the gifts of everlasting life and everlasting love with the world . . . and with you. If you make mistakes, He'll still be your friend. If you behave badly, He'll still love you. If you feel sorry or sad, He can help you feel better.

Jesus wants you to have a happy, healthy life. He wants you to be generous and kind. He wants you to follow His example. And the rest is up to you. You can do it! And with a friend like Jesus, you will.

## A Timely Tip for Girls

Jesus is your true friend. He loves you, and He offers you eternal life with Him in heaven. Welcome Him into your heart. Now!

## More from God's Word

*I have come as a light into the world, so that everyone who believes in Me would not remain in darkness.*

**John 12:46 HCSB**

*We have seen it and we testify and declare to you the eternal life that was with the Father and was revealed to us—what we have seen and heard we also declare to you, so that you may have fellowship along with us; and indeed our fellowship is with the Father and with His Son Jesus Christ.*

**1 John 1:2-4 HCSB**

*Jesus Christ is the same yesterday, today, and forever.*

**Hebrews 13:8 HCSB**

## A Timely Tip for Moms

Jesus is the light of the world. As a caring parent, it's up to you to make certain that He's the light of your family, too.

## Some Very Bright Ideas

In the dark? Follow the Son.

**Anonymous**

Jesus Christ is the One by Whom, for Whom, through Whom everything was made. Therefore, He knows what's wrong in your life, and He knows how to fix it.

**Anne Graham Lotz**

Tell me the story of Jesus. Write on my heart every word. Tell me the story most precious, sweetest that ever was heard.

**Fanny Crosby**

## A Mother-Daughter Prayer

*Dear Lord, we know that Jesus loves us. Please let us share His love with others so that through us, people can understand what it means to follow Christ. Amen*

# Starting Your Day with God

*It is good to give thanks to the Lord, to sing praises to the Most High. It is good to proclaim your unfailing love in the morning, your faithfulness in the evening.*

**Psalm 92:1-2 NLT**

How do you start your day? Do you sleep until the last possible moment and then hop out of bed without giving a single thought to God? Hopefully not. If you're smart, you'll start your day with a prayer of thanks to your Heavenly Father.

Each new day is a gift from God, and if you're wise, you'll spend a few quiet moments thanking the Giver. It's a wonderful way to start your day.

## A Timely Tip for Girls

Make an appointment with God every day, and keep it. Reading your Bible and saying your prayers are important things to do. Very important. So please don't forget to talk with God every day.

# More from God's Word

*Morning by morning he wakens me and opens my understanding to his will. The Sovereign Lord has spoken to me, and I have listened.*

**Isaiah 50:4-5 NLT**

*Be still, and know that I am God.*

**Psalm 46:10 NKJV**

*But grow in the grace and knowledge of our Lord and Savior Jesus Christ. To Him be the glory both now and to the day of eternity.*

**2 Peter 3:18 HCSB**

# A Timely Tip for Moms

Daily devotionals never go out of style. Are you too busy for a daily devotional with your family? If so, it's time to reorder your priorities.

## Some Very Bright Ideas

A person with no devotional life generally struggles with faith and obedience.

**Charles Stanley**

Think of this—we may live together with Him here and now, a daily walking with Him who loved us and gave Himself for us.

**Elisabeth Elliot**

Even Jesus, clear as he was about his calling, had to get his instructions once day at a time. One time he was told to wait, another time to go.

**Laurie Beth Jones**

## A Mother-Daughter Prayer

*Dear Lord, the Bible teaches us that we should turn to You often, and that's what we will do today and every day. Amen*

# Sharing

*If you have two shirts, share with the person who does not have one. If you have food, share that too.*

**Luke 3:11 ICB**

How many times have you heard someone say, "Don't touch that; it's mine!" If you're like most of us, you've heard those words many times and you may have even said them yourself.

The Bible tells us that it's better for us to share things than it is to keep them all to ourselves. And the Bible also tells us that when we share, it's best to do so cheerfully. So be sure to share. It's the best way because it's God's way.

## A Timely Tip for Girls

Your acts of kindness and generosity will speak far louder than words.

## More from God's Word

*The one who has two shirts must share with someone who has none, and the one who has food must do the same.*

**Luke 3:11 HCSB**

*Take heed that you do not do your charitable deeds before men, to be seen by them. Otherwise you have no reward in heaven.*

**Matthew 6:1 NKJV**

*If a brother or sister is without clothes and lacks daily food, and one of you says to them, "Go in peace, keep warm, and eat well," but you don't give them what the body needs, what good is it?*

**James 2:15–16 HCSB**

## A Timely Tip for Moms

It's almost Biblical: when two or more small children are gathered together, they are bound to fuss over toys. Use these disagreements as opportunities to preach the gospel of sharing (even if your sermon falls upon inattentive little ears!).

## Some Very Bright Ideas

We are never more like God than when we give.

**Charles Swindoll**

The happiest and most joyful people are those who give.

**Dave Ramsey**

Don't be afraid to share what you have with others; after all, it all belongs to God anyway.

**Jim Gallery**

Abundant living means abundant giving.

**E. Stanley Jones**

## A Mother-Daughter Prayer

*Dear Lord, let us find ways to help other people. Jesus served others; we can too. We can share our possessions and our prayers. And, we can share kind words with our family and friends, today and every day. Amen*

# It's Easy to Worry

*The Lord himself will go before you. He will be with you; he will not leave you or forget you. Don't be afraid and don't worry.*

**Deuteronomy 31:8 NCV**

It's easy to worry about things—big things and little things. But the Bible promises us that if we learn to trust God more and more each day, we won't worry so much.

Are you worried about something? If so, try doing these two things: first, ask God for His help. And second, talk things over with your parents. When you do these things, you won't worry so much. And that's good . . . VERY good!

## A Timely Tip for Girls

Worried about something you said or did? If you made a mistake yesterday, the day to fix it is today. Then, you won't have to worry about it tomorrow.

# More from God's Word

*Don't worry about anything, but in everything, through prayer and petition with thanksgiving, let your requests be made known to God.*

**Philippians 4:6 HCSB**

*Therefore don't worry about tomorrow, because tomorrow will worry about itself. Each day has enough trouble of its own.*

**Matthew 6:34 HCSB**

*Yea, though I walk through the valley of the shadow of death, I will fear no evil: for thou art with me; thy rod and thy staff they comfort me.*

**Psalm 23:4 KJV**

## A Timely Tip for Moms

If you're worried about your future, your family, or anything else, for that matter, pray about it. God is bigger than your problems.

## Some Very Bright Ideas

Any concern that is too small to be turned into a prayer is too small to be made into a burden.

**Corrie ten Boom**

The things that you worry about most are also the things you should pray about most.

**Criswell Freeman**

Because God is my sovereign Lord, I was not worried. He manages perfectly, day and night, year in and year out, the movements of the stars, the wheeling of the planets, the staggering coordination of events that goes on at the molecular level in order to hold things together. There is no doubt that he can manage the timing of my days and weeks.

**Elisabeth Elliot**

## A Mother-Daughter Prayer

*Dear Lord, when we are discouraged or afraid, we can always talk to You. We thank You for Your love, Father . . . and we thank You for our family. Amen*

# Forgive . . . Quickly

*Be even-tempered, content with second place, quick to forgive an offense. Forgive as quickly and completely as the Master forgave you. And regardless of what else you put on, wear love. It's your basic, all-purpose garment. Never be without it.*

**Colossians 3:13-14 MSG**

When you make a mistake or hurt someone's feelings, what should you do? You should say you're sorry and ask for forgiveness. And you should do so sooner, not later.

The longer you wait to apologize, the harder it is on you. So if you've done something wrong, don't be afraid to ask for forgiveness, and don't be afraid to ask for it NOW!

## A Timely Tip for Girls

Forgiving other people is one way of strengthening your relationship with God.

## More from God's Word

*If we say, "We have no sin," we are deceiving ourselves, and the truth is not in us. If we confess our sins, He is faithful and righteous to forgive us our sins and to cleanse us from all unrighteousness.*

**1 John 1:8-9 HCSB**

*All the prophets testify about Him that through His name everyone who believes in Him will receive forgiveness of sins.*

**Acts 10:43 HCSB**

*When Jesus stood up, He said to her, "Woman, where are they? Has no one condemned you?" "No one, Lord," she answered. "Neither do I condemn you," said Jesus. "Go, and from now on do not sin any more."*

**John 8:10-11 HCSB**

## A Timely Tip for Moms

If you want your children to learn the art of forgiveness, then you must master that art yourself. If you're able to forgive those who have hurt you and, by doing so, move on with your life, your kids will learn firsthand that forgiveness is God's way.

## Some Very Bright Ideas

If you can forgive the person you were, accept the person you are, and believe in the person you will become, you are headed for joy. So celebrate your life.

**Barbara Johnson**

God calls upon the loved not just to love but to be loving. God calls upon the forgiven not just to forgive but to be forgiving.

**Beth Moore**

We all agree that forgiveness is a beautiful idea until we have to practice it.

**C. S. Lewis**

## A Mother-Daughter Prayer

*Dear Lord, when we make mistakes, help us be quick to admit them, quick to correct them, and quick to ask for forgiveness. Amen*

# Friends Are a Good Thing

*If you've gotten anything at all out of following Christ, if his love has made any difference in your life, if being in a community of the Spirit means anything to you, if you have a heart, if you care—then do me a favor: Agree with each other, love each other, be deep-spirited friends.*

**Philippians 2:1-2 MSG**

The Bible tells us that friendship can be a wonderful thing. That's why it's good to know how to make and to keep good friends.

If you want to make lots of friends, practice the Golden Rule with everybody you know. Be kind. Share. Say nice things. Be helpful. When you do, you'll discover that the Golden Rule isn't just a nice way to behave; it's also a great way to make and to keep friends!

## A Timely Tip for Girls

If you want to make more friends, how can you do it? Try this: First, become more interested in them . . . and pretty soon they'll become more interested in you!

# More from God's Word

*As iron sharpens iron, a friend sharpens a friend.*
**Proverbs 27:17 NLT**

*Beloved, if God so loved us, we also ought to love one another.*
**1 John 4:11 NKJV**

*This is my command: Love one another the way I loved you. This is the very best way to love. Put your life on the line for your friends.*
**John 15:12-13 MSG**

# A Timely Tip for Moms

As parents, we can't make friendships for our children, but we can coach them on the art of making friends. All of us, whether youngsters or grown-ups, make friends by treating others as we wish to be treated. And if that sounds suspiciously like the Golden Rule, that's because it is the Golden Rule.

## Some Very Bright Ideas

When friends meet, hearts warm.

**Anonymous**

Inasmuch as anyone pushes you nearer to God, he or she is your friend.

**Barbara Johnson**

If you choose friends wisely, you'll soon be blessed. If you choose friends unwisely, you'll soon be in a mess.

**Criswell Freeman**

## A Mother-Daughter Prayer

*Dear Lord, we thank You for our friends. Please let us be trustworthy friends to other people, and let our friends know how much we love them. Amen*

# Share Your Blessings

*Remember this: the person who sows sparingly will also reap sparingly, and the person who sows generously will also reap generously.*

**2 Corinthians 9:6 HCSB**

Jesus told us that we should be generous with other people, but sometimes we don't feel much like sharing. Instead of sharing the things that we have, we want to keep them all to ourselves. But God doesn't want selfishness to rule our hearts; He wants us to be generous.

Are you lucky enough to have nice things? If so, God's instructions are clear: you must share your blessings with others. And that's exactly the way it should be. After all, think how generous God has been with you.

## A Timely Tip for Girls

There is a direct relationship between generosity and joy—the more you give to others, the more joy you will experience for yourself.

## More from God's Word

*When it is in your power, don't withhold good from the one to whom it is due.*

**Proverbs 3:27 HCSB**

*So whenever you give to the poor, don't sound a trumpet before you, as the hypocrites do in the synagogues and on the streets, to be applauded by people. I assure you: They've got their reward! But when you give to the poor, don't let your left hand know what your right hand is doing, so that your giving may be in secret. And your Father who sees in secret will reward you.*

**Matthew 6:2-4 HCSB**

*A generous person will be enriched.*

**Proverbs 11:25 HCSB**

## A Timely Tip for Moms

It's never too early to emphasize the importance of giving. From the time that a child is old enough to drop a penny into the offering plate, we, as parents, should stress the obligation that we all have to share the blessings that God has shared with us.

# Never-Ending Love

*The unfailing love of the Lord never ends!*

**Lamentations 3:22 NLT**

How much does God love you? He loves you so much that He sent His Son Jesus to come to this earth for you! And, when you accept Jesus into your heart, God gives you a gift that is more precious than gold: that gift is called "eternal life" which means that you will live forever with God in heaven!

God's love is bigger and more powerful than anybody can imagine, but it is very real. So do yourself a favor right now: accept God's love with open arms and welcome His Son Jesus into your heart. When you do, your life will be changed today, tomorrow, and forever.

## A Timely Tip for Girls

When you learn about the Bible, you'll learn how much God loves you.

# More from God's Word

*We know how much God loves us, and we have put our trust in him. God is love, and all who live in love live in God, and God lives in them.*

**1 John 4:16 NLT**

*As the Father loved Me, I also have loved you; abide in My love.*

**John 15:9 NKJV**

*For God so loved the world, that he gave his only begotten Son, that whosoever believeth in him should not perish, but have everlasting life.*

**John 3:16 KJV**

## A Timely Tip for Moms

You know that "God is love." Now, it's your responsibility to make certain that your children know it, too.

## Some Very Bright Ideas

As God's children, we are the recipients of lavish love—a love that motivates us to keep trusting even when we have no idea what God is doing.

**Beth Moore**

Nails didn't hold Jesus on the cross. His love for you did.

**Anonymous**

You and I need to learn to interpret our circumstances by His love, not interpret His love by our circumstances!

**Anne Graham Lotz**

## A Mother-Daughter Prayer

*Dear God, we know that Your love lasts forever. We thank You, Father, for Your amazing love. Every day, we will share Your love with others, and we will do our best to walk in the footsteps of Your Son. Amen*

# Christ's Peace

*Peace I leave with you. My peace I give to you. I do not give to you as the world gives. Your heart must not be troubled or fearful.*

**John 14:27 HCSB**

The beautiful words of John 14:27 remind us that Jesus offers us peace, not as the world gives, but as He alone gives. We, as believers, can accept His peace or ignore it. When we accept the peace of Jesus Christ into our hearts, our lives are changed forever, and we become more loving, patient Christians.

Christ's peace is offered freely; it has been already been paid for; it is ours for the asking. So let us ask . . . and then share.

## A Timely Tip for Girls

Genuine peace is a gift from God. Your job is to accept it.

## More from God's Word

*The result of righteousness will be peace; the effect of righteousness will be quiet confidence forever.*

**Isaiah 32:17 HCSB**

*Peace, peace to you, and peace to him who helps you, for your God helps you.*

**1 Chronicles 12:18 HCSB**

*Grace, mercy, and peace will be with us from God the Father and from Jesus Christ, the Son of the Father, in truth and love.*

**2 John 1:3 HCSB**

## A Timely Tip for Moms

Peace begins at home. As the parent, you're in charge of keeping the peace and sharing it. It's a big job, so don't be afraid to ask for help . . . especially God's help.

## Some Very Bright Ideas

Peace is full confidence that God is Who He says He is and that He will keep every promise in His Word.

**Dorothy Harrison Pentecost**

We must learn to move according to the timetable of the Timeless One, and to be at peace.

**Elisabeth Elliot**

There is never any peace for those who resist God.

**François Fènelon**

## A Mother-Daughter Prayer

*Dear Lord, You know our hearts. Help us to say things, to do things, and to think things that are pleasing to You. Amen*

# Is the Golden Rule Your Rule, Too?

*Don't be selfish…. Be humble, thinking of others as better than yourself.*

**Philippians 2:3 TLB**

Is the Golden Rule your rule, or is it just another Bible verse that goes in one ear and out the other? Jesus made Himself perfectly clear: He instructed you to treat other people in the same way that you want to be treated. But sometimes, especially when you're feeling pressure from friends, or when you're tired or upset, obeying the Golden Rule can seem like an impossible task—but it's not. So be kind to everybody and obey God's rule, the Golden Rule, that is.

## A Timely Tip for Girls

You must do more than talk about it. In order to be a good person, you must do good things. So get busy! The best time to do a good deed is as soon as you can do it!

# More from God's Word

*Each of you should look not only to your own interests, but also to the interest of others.*

**Philippians 2:4 NIV**

*Carry each other's burdens, and in this way you will fulfill the law of Christ.*

**Galatians 6:2 NIV**

*See that no one renders evil for evil to anyone, but always pursue what is good both for yourselves and for all.*

**1 Thessalonians 5:15 NKJV**

## A Timely Tip for Moms

The Golden Rule . . . is as good as gold—in fact, it's better than gold. And as a responsible parent, you should make certain that your child knows that the Golden Rule is, indeed, golden.

## Some Very Bright Ideas

The Golden Rule starts at home, but it should never stop there.

**Marie T. Freeman**

To keep the Golden Rule we must put ourselves in other people's places, but to do that consists in and depends upon picturing ourselves in their places.

**Harry Emerson Fosdick**

It is wrong for anyone to be anxious to receive more from his neighbor than he himself is willing to give to God.

**St. Francis of Assisi**

## A Mother-Daughter Prayer

*Dear Lord, the Golden Rule is Your rule. Today and every day, we will try to make it our rule, too. Amen*

# The Habit of Honesty

*Those who want to do right more than anything else are happy. God will fully satisfy them.*

**Matthew 5:6 ICB**

Our lives are made up of lots and lots of habits. And the habits we choose help determine the kind of people we become. If we choose habits that are good, we are happier and healthier. If we choose habits that are bad, then it's too bad for us!

Honesty, like so many other things, is a habit. And it's a habit that is right for you.

Do you want to grow up to become the kind of woman that God intends for you to be? Then get into the habit of being honest with everybody. You'll be glad you did . . . and so will God!

## A Timely Tip for Girls

When telling the truth is hard, that probably means that you're afraid of what others might think—or what they might do—when you're truthful. Remember that it is usually better to face those kinds of problems now rather than later!

## More from God's Word

*For there is nothing covered, that shall not be revealed; neither hid, that shall not be known. Therefore, whatsoever ye have spoken in darkness shall be heard in the light; and that which ye have spoken in the ear in closets shall be proclaimed upon the housetops.*

**Luke 12:2-3 KJV**

*Ye shall not steal, neither deal falsely, neither lie one to another.*
**Leviticus 19:11 KJV**

*So put away all falsehood and "tell your neighbor the truth" because we belong to each other.*

**Ephesians 4:25 NLT**

## A Timely Tip for Moms

Telling the truth isn't just hard for kids; it can be hard for parents, too. And when honesty is hard for you, that's precisely the moment when wise parents remember that their children are watching . . . and learning.

## Some Very Bright Ideas

If you want to form a new habit, get to work. If you want to break a bad habit, get on your knees.

**Marie T. Freeman**

Falsehood is cowardice, the truth courage.

**Hosea Ballou**

You cannot glorify Christ and practice deception at the same time.

**Warren Wiersbe**

## A Mother-Daughter Prayer

*Dear Lord, we know that it's good to be honest. So please help us form the habit of being honest with everybody, even when it's hard. Amen*

# Don't Whine!

*Words kill, words give life; they're either poison or fruit—you choose.*

**Proverbs 18:21 MSG**

Do you like to listen to other children whine? No way! And since you don't like to hear other kids whining, then you certainly shouldn't whine, either.

Sometimes, kids think that whining is a good way to get the things they want . . . but it's not! So if your parents or your teacher ask you to do something, don't complain about it. And if there's something you want, don't whine and complain until you get it.

Remember: whining won't make you happy . . . and it won't make anybody else happy, either.

## A Timely Tip for Girls

Whining can be contagious, so make sure that your home is, to the greatest extent possible, a whine-free zone. How can you do this? A good way to start is by counting your blessings, not your problems.

# More from God's Word

*Friends, don't complain about each other. A far greater complaint could be lodged against you, you know. The Judge is standing just around the corner.*

**James 5:9 MSG**

*Do everything without complaining or arguing. Then you will be innocent and without any wrong.*

**Philippians 2:14-15 NCV**

*May the words of my mouth and the thoughts of my heart be pleasing to you, O LORD, my rock and my redeemer.*

**Psalm 19:14 NLT**

# A Timely Tip for Moms

Whining can be contagious, so make sure that your home is, to the greatest extent possible, a whine-free zone. How can you do this? A good way to start is by counting your blessings, not your problems.

## Some Very Bright Ideas

It's your choice: you can either count your blessings or recount your disappointments.

**Jim Gallery**

He wants us to have a faith that does not complain while waiting, but rejoices because we know our times are in His hands—nail-scarred hands that labor for our highest good.

**Kay Arthur**

Jesus wept, but he never complained.

**C. H. Spurgeon**

## A Mother-Daughter Prayer

*Dear Lord, let us count our blessings and be thankful. And help us remember not to whine about the things we don't have. Amen*

# A Fruitful Friendship

*I am the Vine, you are the branches. When you're joined with me and I with you, the relation intimate and organic, the harvest is sure to be abundant.*

**John 15:5 MSG**

Whether you realize it or not, you already have a relationship with Jesus. Hopefully, it's a close relationship! Why? Because the friendship you form with Jesus will help you every day of your life . . . and beyond!

You can either choose to invite Him into your heart, or you can ignore Him altogether. Welcome Him today—and while you're at it, encourage your friends and family members to do the same.

## A Timely Tip for Girls

What a friend you have in Jesus: Jesus loves you, and He offers you eternal life with Him in heaven. Welcome Him into your heart. Now!

# More from God's Word

*Jesus Christ is the same yesterday, today, and forever.*

**Hebrews 13:8 HCSB**

*I am the true vine, and My Father is the vineyard keeper. Every branch in Me that does not produce fruit He removes, and He prunes every branch that produces fruit so that it will produce more fruit.*

**John 15:1-2 HCSB**

*I have come as a light into the world, so that everyone who believes in Me would not remain in darkness.*

**John 12:46 HCSB**

## A Timely Tip for Moms

Jesus loves you, and He offers you eternal life with Him in heaven. Welcome Him into your heart. Now! For your children's sake.

# Some Very Bright Ideas

I am truly happy with Jesus Christ. I couldn't live without Him. When my life gets beyond the ability to cope, He takes over.

**Ruth Bell Graham**

Christians see sin for what it is: willful rebellion against the rulership of God in their lives. And in turning from their sin, they have embraced God's only means of dealing with sin: Jesus.

**Kay Arthur**

He is the door of the greatest temple. He is the way of life. He is the guide to salvation. He is the gate of life.

**Lactantius**

# A Mother-Daughter Prayer

*Dear Jesus, we know that You love us today and that You will love us forever. And, we thank You for Your love . . . today and forever. Amen*

# Be Respectful

*Show respect for all people. Love the brothers and sisters of God's family.*

**1 Peter 2:17 ICB**

A re you polite and respectful to your parents and teachers? And do you do your best to treat everybody with the respect they deserve? If you want to obey God's rules, then you should be able to answer yes to these questions.

Remember this: the Bible teaches you to be a respectful person—and if it's right there in the Bible, it's certainly the right thing to do!

## A Timely Tip for Girls

If you're angry with your mom or your dad, don't blurt out something unkind. If you can't say anything nice, go to your room and don't come out until you can.

# More from God's Word

*Be completely humble and gentle; be patient, bearing with one another in love.*

**Ephesians 4:2 NIV**

*Wherefore seeing we also are compassed about with so great a cloud of witnesses, let us lay aside every weight, and the sin which doth so easily beset us, and let us run with patience the race that is set before us....*

**Hebrews 12:1 KJV**

*Encourage each other. Live in harmony and peace. Then the God of love and peace will be with you.*

**2 Corinthians 13:11 NLT**

# A Timely Tip for Moms

Kindness, dignity, and respect for others begins at the head of the household and works its way down from there.

## Some Very Bright Ideas

If you are willing to honor a person out of respect for God, you can be assured that God will honor you.

**Beth Moore**

If my heart is right with God, every human being is my neighbor.

**Oswald Chambers**

Use your head to handle yourself, your heart to handle others.

**Anonymous**

## A Mother-Daughter Prayer

*Dear Lord, please give us the maturity to respect other people, today and every day. Amen*

# Slow Down!

*Knowing God leads to self-control. Self-control leads to patient endurance, and patient endurance leads to godliness.*

**2 Peter 1:6 NLT**

**M**aybe you're one of those girls who tries to do everything fast, faster, or fastest! If so, maybe you sometimes do things before you think about the consequences of your actions. If that's the case, it's probably a good idea to slow down a little bit so you can think before you act. When you do, you'll soon discover the value of thinking carefully about things before you get started. And while you're at it, it's probably a good idea to think before you speak, too. After all, you'll never have to apologize for something that you didn't say.

## A Timely Tip for Girls

If you learn to control yourself, you'll be glad. If you can't learn to control yourself, you'll be sad.

## More from God's Word

*So prepare your minds for service and have self-control.*

**1 Peter 1:13 NCV**

*Discipline yourself for the purpose of godliness.*

**1 Timothy 4:7 NASB**

*So don't lose a minute in building on what you've been given, complementing your basic faith with good character, spiritual understanding, alert discipline, passionate patience, reverent wonder, warm friendliness, and generous love, each dimension fitting into and developing the others.*

**2 Peter 1:5-7 MSG**

## A Timely Tip for Moms

Be an example of self-control. When it comes to parenting, you can't really teach it if you won't really live it.

## Some Very Bright Ideas

We are so used to living in an instant world that it is difficult to wait for anything.

**Kay Arthur**

If only we could be as patient with other people as God is with us!

**Jim Gallery**

Patience pays. Impatience costs.

**Criswell Freeman**

## A Mother-Daughter Prayer

*Dear Lord, today and every day, we ask that You help us slow down and think about things before we do them. And, when we slow down to think about things, help us discover ways to follow in the footsteps of Your Son. Amen*

# The Courage to Tell the Truth

*And you shall know the truth, and the truth shall make you free.*

**John 8:32 NKJV**

Sometimes, we're afraid of what might happen if we tell the truth. And sometimes, instead of doing the courageous thing, we do the unwise thing: we lie.

When we're fearful, we can and should find strength from friends, from family members, and from God.

So if you're afraid to tell the truth, don't be! Keep looking until you find the courage to be honest. Then, you'll discover it's not the truth that you should be afraid of; it's those troublesome, pesky lies!

## A Timely Tip for Girls

Never be afraid to tell the truth. Even when the truth hurts, telling the truth is better than telling a lie. Far better!

## More from God's Word

*So put away all falsehood and "tell your neighbor the truth" because we belong to each other.*

**Ephesians 4:25 NLT**

*For there is nothing covered, that shall not be revealed; neither hid, that shall not be known. Therefore, whatsoever ye have spoken in darkness shall be heard in the light; and that which ye have spoken in the ear in closets shall be proclaimed upon the housetops.*

**Luke 12:2-3 KJV**

*Ye shall not steal, neither deal falsely, neither lie one to another.*

**Leviticus 19:11 KJV**

## A Timely Tip for Moms

In every family, truth starts at the top. So live your life—and raise your kids—accordingly.

## Some Very Bright Ideas

A person who really cares about his or her neighbor, a person who genuinely loves others, is a person who bears witness to the truth.

**Anne Graham Lotz**

Integrity is the glue that holds our way of life together. We must constantly strive to keep our integrity intact.

**Billy Graham**

Honesty is a sign of maturity.

**Charles Swindoll**

## A Mother-Daughter Prayer

*Dear Lord, sometimes it's hard to tell the truth. When we are fearful of telling the truth, give us the courage to do what's right. Give us the courage to be truthful. Amen*

# The Words You Speak

*If anyone considers himself religious and yet does not keep a tight rein on his tongue, he deceives himself and his religion is worthless.*

**James 1:26 NIV**

The words you speak are important. If you speak kind words, you make other people feel better. And that's exactly what you should do!

How hard is it to say a kind word? Not very! Yet sometimes we're so busy that we forget to say the very things that might make other people feel better.

Kind words help; cruel words hurt. It's as simple as that. And, when we say the right thing at the right time, we give a gift that can change somebody's day or somebody's life.

## A Timely Tip for Girls

If you're not sure that it's the right thing to say, don't say it! And if you're not sure that it's the truth, don't tell it.

## More from God's Word

*Avoid irreverent, empty speech, for this will produce an even greater measure of godlessness.*

**2 Timothy 2:16 HCSB**

*Therefore, laying aside all malice, all deceit, hypocrisy, envy, and all evil speaking, as newborn babes, desire the pure milk of the word, that you may grow thereby.*

**1 Peter 2:1-2 NKJV**

*Finally, all of you be of one mind, having compassion for one another; love as brothers, be tenderhearted, be courteous.*

**1 Peter 3:8 NKJV**

## A Timely Tip for Moms

Words, words, words . . . are important, important, important! And, some of the most important words you will ever speak are the ones that your children hear. So whether or not you are talking directly to your kids, choose your words carefully.

## Some Very Bright Ideas

We will always experience regret when we live for the moment and do not weigh our words and deeds before we give them life.

**Lisa Bevere**

When you talk, choose the very same words that you would use if Jesus were looking over your shoulder. Because He is.

**Marie T. Freeman**

It is time that the followers of Jesus revise their language and learn to speak respectfully of non-Christian peoples.

**Lottie Moon**

## A Mother-Daughter Prayer

*Dear Lord, we know that the words we speak are important. Today, help us think about our words before we say them, not after. Amen*

# Everlasting Protection

*The Lord is my rock, my fortress, and my deliverer, my God, my mountain where I seek refuge. My shield, the horn of my salvation, my stronghold, my refuge, and my Savior.*

**2 Samuel 22:2-3 HCSB**

Life isn't always easy. Far from it! Sometimes, life can be very hard indeed. But even when we're upset or hurt, we must remember that we're protected by a loving Heavenly Father.

When we're worried, God can reassure us; when we're sad, God can comfort us. When our feelings are hurt, God is not just near, He is here. We must lift our thoughts and prayers to our Father in heaven. When we do, He will answer our prayers. Why? Because He is our Shepherd, and He has promised to protect us now and forever.

## A Timely Tip for Girls

The best protection comes from the loving heart of God—and from the salvation that flows from His only begotten Son.

# More from God's Word

*Finally, my brethren, be strong in the Lord and in the power of His might. Put on the whole armor of God, that you may be able to stand against the wiles of the devil.*

**Ephesians 6:10-11 NKJV**

*The Lord your God in your midst, The Mighty One, will save; He will rejoice over you with gladness, He will quiet you with His love, He will rejoice over you with singing.*

**Zephaniah 3:17 NKJV**

*God is my shield, saving those whose hearts are true and right.*

**Psalm 7:10 NLT**

## A Timely Tip for Moms

Remember that God protects you, too! So if you're feeling a little apprehensive about the future, fear not. God promises to protect every member of your family, and that includes you!

## Some Very Bright Ideas

The task ahead of us is never as great as the Power behind us.

**Anonymous**

God will never let you sink under your circumstances. He always provides a safety net and His love always encircles.

**Barbara Johnson**

He goes before us, follows behind us, and hems us safe inside the realm of His protection.

**Beth Moore**

## A Mother-Daughter Prayer

*Dear Lord, because You watch over us, we don't have to be afraid. Because You are with us always, we can have hope. Thank You, Lord, for protecting us today, tomorrow, and forever. Amen*

# No More Tantrums

*A patient person [shows] great understanding. but a quick-tempered one promotes foolishness.*

**Proverbs 14:29 HCSB**

Temper tantrums are so silly. And so is pouting. So, of course, is whining. When we lose our tempers, we say things that we shouldn't say, and we do things that we shouldn't do. Too bad!

The Bible tells us that it is foolish to become angry and that it is wise to remain calm. That's why we should learn to control our tempers before our tempers control us.

### A Timely Tip for Girls

If you think you're about to pitch a fit or throw a tantrum, slow down, catch your breath, and walk away if you must. It's better to walk away—and keep walking—than it is to blurt out angry words that can't be un-blurted.

# More from God's Word

*Don't let your spirit rush to be angry, for anger abides in the heart of fools.*

**Ecclesiastes 7:9 HCSB**

*My dearly loved brothers, understand this: everyone must be quick to hear, slow to speak, and slow to anger, for man's anger does not accomplish God's righteousness.*

**James 1:19-20 HCSB**

*A fool's displeasure is known at once, but whoever ignores an insult is sensible.*

**Proverbs 12:16 HCSB**

## A Timely Tip for Moms

When your children become angry or upset, you'll tend to become angry and upset, too. Resist that temptation. As the grown-up person in the family, it's up to you to remain calm, even when other, less mature members of the family can't.

## Some Very Bright Ideas

Life is too short to spend it being angry, bored, or dull.

**Barbara Johnson**

If your temper gets the best of you . . . then other people get to see the worst in you.

**Marie T. Freeman**

Why lose your temper if, by doing so, you offend God, annoy other people, give yourself a bad time . . . and, in the end, have to find it again?

**Josemaria Escriva**

## A Mother-Daughter Prayer

*Dear Lord, You know that we can be impatient at times. And sometimes, we become angry. When we become upset, please calm us down, Lord, and help us forgive the people who have made us angry. We know that Jesus forgave other people, and we should, too. Amen*

# Patience and Love

*I wait for the Lord; I wait, and put my hope in His word.*

**Psalm 130:5 HCSB**

God has a perfect idea of the kind of people He wants us to become. And for starters, He wants us to be loving, kind, and patient—not rude or mean!

The Bible tells us that God is love and that if we wish to know Him, we must have love in our hearts. Sometimes, of course, when we're tired, angry, or frustrated, it is very hard for us to be loving. Thankfully, anger and frustration are feelings that come and go, but God's love lasts forever.

If you'd like to become a more patient girl, talk to God in prayer, listen to what He says, and share His love with your family and friends. God is always listening, and He's ready to talk to you . . . now!

## A Timely Tip for Girls

God has been patient with you . . . now it's your turn to be patient with others.

# More from God's Word

*Knowing God leads to self-control. Self-control leads to patient endurance, and patient endurance leads to godliness.*

**2 Peter 1:6 NLT**

*Patience and encouragement come from God. And I pray that God will help you all agree with each other the way Christ Jesus wants.*

**Romans 15:5 NCV**

*But if we look forward to something we don't have yet, we must wait patiently and confidently.*

**Romans 8:25 NLT**

## A Timely Tip for Moms

Kids imitate their parents, so act accordingly! The best way for your child to learn to be patient is by example . . . your example!

## Some Very Bright Ideas

He makes us wait. He keeps us in the dark on purpose. He makes us walk when we want to run, sit still when we want to walk, for he has things to do in our souls that we are not interested in.

**Elisabeth Elliot**

Those who have had to wait and work for happiness seem to enjoy it more, because they never take it for granted.

**Barbara Johnson**

Waiting means going about our assigned tasks, confident that God will provide the meaning and the conclusions.

**Eugene Peterson**

## A Mother-Daughter Prayer

*Dear Lord, sometimes we are not as patient as we could be, or as patient as we should be. Please slow us down, Lord. And teach us to follow in the footsteps of Your Son today and every day. Amen*

# Know When to Say No

*Wisdom will save you from the ways of wicked men....*

**Proverbs 2:12 NIV**

It happens to all of us at one time or another: a friend asks us to do something that we think is wrong. What should we do? Should we try to please our friend by doing something bad? No way! It's not worth it!

Trying to please our friends is okay. What's not okay is misbehaving in order to do so. Do you have a friend who encourages you to misbehave? Hopefully you don't have any friends like that. But if you do, say, "No, NO, NOOOOOO!" And what if your friend threatens to break up the friendship? Let her! Friendships like that just aren't worth it.

## A Timely Tip for Girls

Face facts: since you can't please everybody, you're better off trying to please the people who are trying to help you become a better person, not the people who are encouraging you to misbehave!

## More from God's Word

*Do not be misled: "Bad company corrupts good character."*

**1 Corinthians 15:33 NIV**

*Don't become partners with those who reject God. How can you make a partnership out of right and wrong? That's not partnership; that's war. Is light best friends with dark?*

**2 Corinthians 6:14 MSG**

*Friend, don't go along with evil. Model the good. The person who does good does God's work. The person who does evil falsifies God, doesn't know the first thing about God.*

**3 John 1:11 MSG**

## A Timely Tip for Moms

Thoughtful Christian parents don't follow the crowd . . . thoughtful Christian parents follow Jesus.

## Some Very Bright Ideas

You will get untold flak for prioritizing God's revealed and present will for your life over man's . . . but, boy, is it worth it.

**Beth Moore**

We, as God's people, are not only to stay far away from sin and sinners who would entice us, but we are to be so like our God that we mourn over sin.

**Kay Arthur**

True friends will always lift you higher and challenge you to walk in a manner pleasing to our Lord.

**Lisa Bevere**

## A Mother-Daughter Prayer

*Dear Lord, help us worry less about pleasing other people and more about pleasing You. Amen*

# Respect for Others

*Being respected is more important than having great riches.*

**Proverbs 22:1 ICB**

D o you try to have a respectful attitude towards everybody? Hopefully so!

Should you be respectful of grown ups? Of course. Teachers? Certainly. Family members? Yes. Friends? Yep, but it doesn't stop there. The Bible teaches us to treat all people with respect.

Respect for others is habit-forming: the more you do it, the easier it becomes. So start practicing right now. Say lots of kind words and do lots of kind things, because when it comes to kindness and respect, practice makes perfect.

## A Timely Tip for Girls

How did Jesus treat the poor people? And how did He treat people who lived on the edges of society? With patience, respect, and love.

# More from God's Word

*Therefore, God's chosen ones, holy and loved, put on heartfelt compassion, kindness, humility, gentleness, and patience.*
**Colossians 3:12 HCSB**

*Reverence for the Lord is the foundation of true wisdom. The rewards of wisdom come to all who obey him.*
**Psalm 111:10 NLT**

*Acquire wisdom—how much better it is than gold! And acquire understanding—it is preferable to silver.*
**Proverbs 16:16 HCSB**

## A Timely Tip for Moms

How did Jesus treat the people who lived on the edges of society? With patience, respect, and love. And that's precisely the behavior that we must model for our children.

## Some Very Bright Ideas

If we have the true love of God in our hearts, we will show it in our lives. We will not have to go up and down the earth proclaiming it. We will show it in everything we say or do.

**D. L. Moody**

When we do little acts of kindness that make life more bearable for someone else, we are walking in love as the Bible commands us.

**Barbara Johnson**

A little kindly advice is better than a great deal of scolding.

**Fanny Crosby**

## A Mother-Daughter Prayer

*Dear Lord, help us learn to respect all people, starting with our family and our friends. And help us learn to treat other people in the same way that we want to be treated. Amen*

# Sharing Your Stuff

*In every way I've shown you that by laboring like this, it is necessary to help the weak and to keep in mind the words of the Lord Jesus, for He said, "It is more blessed to give than to receive."*

**Acts 20:35 HCSB**

**A**re you one of those girls who is lucky enough to have a closet filled up with stuff? If so, it's probably time to share some of it.

When your mom or dad says it's time to clean up your closet and give some things away, don't be sad. Instead of whining, think about all the children who could enjoy the things that you don't use very much. And while you're at it, think about what Jesus might tell you to do if He were here. Jesus would tell you to share generously and cheerfully. And that's exactly what you should do!

## A Timely Tip for Girls

Find loving homes for your old clothes and toys. Ask your parents to help you find younger children who need the clothes and toys that you've outgrown.

## More from God's Word

*And above all things have fervent charity among yourselves: for charity shall cover the multitude of sins.*

**1 Peter 4:8 KJV**

*Instruct those who are rich in the present age not to be arrogant or to set their hope on the uncertainty of wealth, but on God, who richly provides us with all things to enjoy. Instruct them to do good, to be rich in good works, to be generous, willing to share.*

**1 Timothy 6:17-18 HCSB**

*Be generous: Invest in acts of charity. Charity yields high returns.*

**Ecclesiastes 11:1 MSG**

## A Timely Tip for Moms

When it comes to charity, consistency matters. Do something every day that helps another person have a better life.

## Some Very Bright Ideas

You can't read the Scriptures without being struck that over 2,500 verses deal with the sick, the hungry, the orphans.

**Tony P. Hall**

I never look at the masses as my responsibility. I look at the individual. I can love only one person at a time. I can feed only one person at a time. Just one, one, one. You get closer to Christ by coming closer to each other.

**Mother Teresa**

Charity is the pure gold which makes us rich in eternal wealth.

**Jean Pierre Camus**

## A Mother-Daughter Prayer

*Dear Lord, You've given our family so much, and we know we are blessed. Yet, there are so many people in this world who need our help. Give us the wisdom to share our blessings; let us be kind, generous, and helpful, this day and every day. Amen*

# He Answers

*For I know the thoughts that I think toward you, says the Lord, thoughts of peace and not of evil, to give you a future and a hope. Then you will call upon Me and go and pray to Me, and I will listen to you.*

**Jeremiah 29:11-12 NKJV**

In case you've been wondering, wonder no more—God does answer your prayers. What God does not do is this: He does not always answer your prayers as soon as you might like, and He does not always answer your prayers by saying "Yes."

God answers prayers not only according to our wishes but also according to His master plan. And guess what? We don't know that plan . . . but we can know the Planner.

Are you praying? Then you can be sure that God is listening. And sometime soon, He'll answer!

## A Timely Tip for Girls

When you are praying, your eyes don't always have to be closed. Of course it's good to close your eyes and bow your head, but you can also offer a quick prayer to God with your eyes open. That means that you can pray any time you want.

# More from God's Word

*The intense prayer of the righteous is very powerful.*
**James 5:16 HCSB**

*Rejoice in hope; be patient in affliction; be persistent in prayer.*
**Romans 12:12 HCSB**

*Let the words of my mouth and the meditation of my heart be acceptable in Your sight, O Lord, my strength and my Redeemer.*
**Psalm 19:14 NKJV**

# A Timely Tip for Moms

Are you ever embarrassed to bow your head in a restaurant? Don't be. It's the people who aren't praying who should be embarrassed!

## Some Very Bright Ideas

You don't need fancy words or religious phrases. Just tell God the way it really is.

**Jim Cymbala**

Always stay connected to people and seek out things that bring you joy. Dream with abandon. Pray confidently.

**Barbara Johnson**

Prayer keeps us in constant communion with God, which is the goal of our entire believing lives.

**Beth Moore**

## A Mother-Daughter Prayer

*Dear Lord, You always hear our prayers. Remind us to pray often about the things we need and the things You want us to have. Amen*

# When Nobody
# Is Watching

*Moderation is better than muscle, self-control better than political power.*

**Proverbs 16:32 MSG**

When your teachers or parents aren't watching, what should you do? The answer is that you should behave exactly like you would if they were watching you. But sometimes, you may be tempted to do otherwise.

When a parent steps away or a teacher looks away, you may be tempted to say something or do something that you would not do if they were standing right beside you. But remember this: when nobody's watching, it's up to you to control yourself. And that's exactly what everybody wants you to do: your teachers want you to control yourself, and so do your parents. And so, by the way, does God.

## A Timely Tip for Girls

If you hear a little voice inside your head telling you that you'll never be good enough . . . don't pay attention to that little voice. God loves you . . . and if you're good enough for God, you're good enough.

## More from God's Word

*God hasn't invited us into a disorderly, unkempt life but into something holy and beautiful—as beautiful on the inside as the outside.*

**1 Thessalonians 4:7 MSG**

*Discipline yourself for the purpose of godliness.*

**1 Timothy 4:7 NASB**

*So don't lose a minute in building on what you've been given, complementing your basic faith with good character, spiritual understanding, alert discipline, passionate patience, reverent wonder, warm friendliness, and generous love, each dimension fitting into and developing the others.*

**2 Peter 1:5-7 MSG**

## A Timely Tip for Moms

If you expect your daughter to have self-control, then you must have it, too. When it comes to parenting, you can't really teach it if you won't really live it.

## Some Very Bright Ideas

God nowhere tells us to give up things for the sake of giving them up. He tells us to give them up for the sake of the only thing worth having—life with Himself.

**Oswald Chambers**

Your thoughts are the determining factor as to whose mold you are conformed to. Control your thoughts and you control the direction of your life.

**Charles Stanley**

This is my song through endless ages: Jesus led me all the way.

**Fanny Crosby**

## A Mother-Daughter Prayer

*Dear Lord, the Bible teaches us to be wise, not foolish. So help us slow down and think things through so we can make better decisions and fewer mistakes. Amen*

# God Wants You to Share

*I will make you into a great nation and I will bless you; I will make your name great, and you will be a blessing. I will bless those who bless you, and whoever curses you I will curse; and all peoples on earth will be blessed through you.*

**Genesis 12:2-3 NIV**

You've heard it plenty of times from your parents and teachers: share your things. But it's important to realize that sharing isn't just something that grown-ups want you to do. It's also something that God wants you to do, too.

The word "possessions" is another way of describing the stuff that belongs to you: your clothes, your toys, your books, and things like that are "your possessions."

Jesus says that you should learn how to share your possessions without feeling bad about it. Sometimes, it's very hard to share and very easy to be stingy. But God wants you to share—and to keep sharing!

## A Timely Tip for Girls

What does the Bible say about sharing our possessions? The Bible answers this question very clearly: when other people need our help, we should gladly share the things we have.

# More from God's Word

*In every way I've shown you that by laboring like this, it is necessary to help the weak and to keep in mind the words of the Lord Jesus, for He said, "It is more blessed to give than to receive."*

**Acts 20:35 HCSB**

*Instruct those who are rich in the present age not to be arrogant or to set their hope on the uncertainty of wealth, but on God, who richly provides us with all things to enjoy. Instruct them to do good, to be rich in good works, to be generous, willing to share.*

**1 Timothy 6:17-18 HCSB**

*The one who blesses others is abundantly blessed; those who help others are helped.*

**Proverbs 11:25 MSG**

## A Timely Tip for Moms

Your children will learn how to treat others by watching you (not by listening to you!). Your acts of kindness and generosity will speak far louder than words.

## Some Very Bright Ideas

Don't be afraid to share what you have with others; after all, it all belongs to God anyway.

**Jim Gallery**

When somebody needs a helping hand, he doesn't need it tomorrow or the next day. He needs it now, and that's exactly when you should offer to help. Good deeds, if they are really good, happen sooner rather than later.

**Marie T. Freeman**

Since you cannot do good to all, you are to pay special regard to those who, by the accidents of time, or place, or circumstances, are brought into closer connection with you.

**St. Augustine**

## A Mother-Daughter Prayer

*Dear Lord, Jesus served others; we can too. So, we will share our possessions and our prayers. And, we will share kind words with our family and our friends. Amen*

**Devo 27**

# Making Things Better

*For out of the overflow of the heart the mouth speaks.*

**Matthew 12:34 NIV**

When we're frustrated or tired, it's easier to speak first and think second. But that's not the best way to talk to other people. The Bible tells us that "a good person's words will help many others." But if our words are to be helpful, we must put some thought into them.

The next time you're tempted to say something unkind, remember that your words can and should be helpful to others, not hurtful. God wants to use you to make this world a better place, and He will use the things that you say to help accomplish that goal . . . if you let Him.

## A Timely Tip for Girls

Words have the power to encourage or discourage others. So watch what you say.

## More from God's Word

*If anyone thinks he is religious, without controlling his tongue but deceiving his heart, his religion is useless.*

**James 1:26 HCSB**

*Watch the way you talk. Let nothing foul or dirty come out of your mouth. Say only what helps, each word a gift.*

**Ephesians 4:29 MSG**

*Discipline yourself for the purpose of godliness.*

**1 Timothy 4:7 NASB**

## A Timely Tip for Moms

Words are important. And as a parent, some of the most important words you will ever speak are the words your child hears. So whether you're talking about Jesus or just about anything else, for that matter, choose your words carefully because you can be sure that your youngster is listening very carefully.

## Some Very Bright Ideas

Fill the heart with the love of Christ so that only truth and purity can come out of the mouth.

**Warren Wiersbe**

The battle of the tongue is won not in the mouth, but in the heart.

**Annie Chapman**

The great test of a man's character is his tongue.

**Oswald Chambers**

## A Mother-Daughter Prayer

*Dear Lord, You hear every word that we say. Help us remember to speak words that are honest, kind, and helpful. Amen*

# God's Power

*I pray…that you may know…his uncomparably great power for us who believe….*

**Ephesians 1:18-19 NIV**

How strong is God? Stronger than anybody can imagine! But even if we can't understand God's power, we can respect His power. And we can be sure that God has the strength to guide us and protect us forever.

The next time you're worried or afraid, remember this: if God is powerful enough to create the universe and everything in it, He's also strong enough to take care of you. Now that's a comforting thought!

## A Timely Tip for Girls

When you place your faith in God, life becomes a grand adventure energized by His power.

# More from God's Word

*But Jesus looked at them and said, "With men this is impossible, but with God all things are possible."*

**Matthew 19:26 HCSB**

*You are the God who works wonders; You revealed Your strength among the peoples.*

**Psalm 77:14 HCSB**

*Ah, Lord God! Behold, You have made the heavens and the earth by Your great power and outstretched arm. There is nothing too hard for You.*

**Jeremiah 32:17 NKJV**

## A Timely Tip for Moms

You know that God is sovereign and that His power is unlimited. Make sure that your daughter knows it, too.

## Some Very Bright Ideas

The power of God through His Spirit will work within us to the degree that we permit it.

**Mrs. Charles E. Cowman**

The greatness of His power to create and design and form and mold and make and build and arrange defies the limits of our imagination. And since He created everything, there is nothing beyond His power to fix or mend or heal or restore.

**Anne Graham Lotz**

If you believe in a God who controls the big things, you have to believe in a God who controls the little things. It is we, of course, to whom things look "little" or "big."

**Elisabeth Elliot**

## A Mother-Daughter Prayer

*Dear God, Your power is far too great for us to understand. But we can sense Your presence and Your love every day of our lives—and that's exactly what we will try to do! Amen*

# Working Together

*Work at getting along with each other and with God. Otherwise you'll never get so much as a glimpse of God.*

**Hebrews 12:14 MSG**

**H**elping other people can be fun! When you help others, you feel better about yourself—and you'll know that God approves of what you're doing.

When you learn how to cooperate with your family and friends, you'll soon discover that it's more fun when everybody works together.

So do everybody a favor: learn better ways to share and better ways to cooperate. It's the right thing to do.

## A Timely Tip for Girls

Cooperation pays. When you cooperate with your friends and family, you'll feel good about yourself—and your family and friends will feel good about you, too.

## More from God's Word

*You're blessed when you can show people how to cooperate instead of compete or fight. That's when you discover who you really are, and your place in God's family.*

**Matthew 5:9 MSG**

*Be kind to each other, tenderhearted, forgiving one another, just as God through Christ has forgiven you.*

**Ephesians 4:32 NLT**

*Carry one another's burdens; in this way you will fulfill the law of Christ.*

**Galatians 6:2 HCSB**

## A Timely Tip for Moms

You know that your children can accomplish much more in life by working cooperatively with others. So it's up to you to teach the fine art of cooperation. And make no mistake: the best way to teach the art of cooperation is by example.

## Some Very Bright Ideas

Coming together is a beginning. Keeping together is progress. Working together is success.

**John Maxwell**

A friend is one who makes me do my best.

**Oswald Chambers**

One person working together doesn't accomplish much. Success is the result of people pulling together to meet common goals.

**John Maxwell**

## A Mother-Daughter Prayer

*Dear Lord, help us learn to be kind, courteous, and cooperative with our family and with our friends. Amen*

# Draw a Picture Together about Helping Others

# Do Good Deeds

*A good person produces good deeds from a good heart, and an evil person produces evil deeds from an evil heart. Whatever is in your heart determines what you say.*

**Luke 6:45 NLT**

It's good to do good deeds. Even when nobody's watching, God is. And God knows whether you've done the right thing or the wrong thing.

So if you're tempted to misbehave when nobody is looking, remember this: There is never a time when "nobody's watching." Somebody is always watching over you—and that Somebody, of course, is your Father in Heaven. Don't let Him down!

## A Timely Tip for Girls

Goodness is as goodness does: In order to be a good person, you must do good things. Thinking about them isn't enough. So get busy! Your family and friends need all the good deeds they can get!

# More from God's Word

*In everything set them an example by doing what is good.*

**Titus 2:7 NIV**

*Abhor that which is evil; cleave to that which is good.*

**Romans 12:9 KJV**

*Do not take revenge, my friends, but leave room for God's wrath, for it is written: "It is mine to avenge; I will repay," says the Lord. On the contrary: "If your enemy is hungry, feed him; if he is thirsty, give him something to drink. In doing this, you will heap burning coals on his head." Do not be overcome by evil, but overcome evil with good.*

**Romans 12:19-21 NIV**

## A Timely Tip for Moms

Christianity is more than a way of worshipping; it's a way of life. For believers—Christian parents and children alike—every day should provide opportunities to honor God by walking in the footsteps of His Son.

## Some Very Bright Ideas

Here lies the tremendous mystery—that God should be all-powerful, yet refuse to coerce. He summons us to cooperation. We are honored in being given the opportunity to participate in his good deeds. Remember how He asked for help in performing his miracles: Fill the water pots, stretch out your hand, distribute the loaves.

**Elisabeth Elliot**

Faith never asks whether good works are to be done, but has done them before there is time to ask the question, and it is always doing them.

**Martin Luther**

All our goodness is a loan; God is the owner.

**St. John of the Cross**

## A Mother-Daughter Prayer

*Dear Lord, when our family or friends need our help, remind us to behave ourselves like the Good Samaritan. Let us be generous, kind, and helpful, Lord, today and every day. Amen*

# The Master Teacher

*This man came to Him at night and said, "Rabbi, we know that You have come from God as a teacher, for no one could perform these signs You do unless God were with him."*

**John 3:2 HCSB**

**W**ho was the greatest teacher in the history of the world? Jesus was . . . and He still is! Jesus teaches us how to live, how to behave, and how to worship. Now, it's up to each of us, as Christians, to learn the important lessons that Jesus can teach.

Some day soon, you will have learned everything that Jesus has to teach you, right? WRONG! Jesus will keep teaching you important lessons throughout your life. And that's good, because all of us, kids and grown-ups alike, have lots to learn . . . especially from the Master . . . and the Master, of course, is Jesus.

## A Timely Tip for Girls

The Truth with a capital "T": Jesus is the Truth, and that's the truth!

## More from God's Word

*Then He said to them all, "If anyone wants to come with Me, he must deny himself, take up his cross daily, and follow Me."*

**Luke 9:23 HCSB**

*Love consists in this: not that we loved God, but that He loved us and sent His Son to be the propitiation for our sins.*

**1 John 4:10 HCSB**

*Therefore if any man be in Christ, he is a new creature: old things are passed away; behold, all things are become new.*

**2 Corinthians 5:17 KJV**

## A Timely Tip for Moms

It's good to talk about Jesus. So family discussions about God and His Son shouldn't be reserved for "special" occasions or Sunday School lessons. Since you're serious about your faith, talk to your kids about it. And when it comes to the marvelous things God has done, speak openly, sincerely, and often.

## Some Very Bright Ideas

There was One, who for "us sinners and our salvation," left the glories of heaven and sojourned upon this earth in weariness and woe, amid those who hated his and finally took his life.

**Lottie Moon**

I am truly happy with Jesus Christ. I couldn't live without Him. When my life gets beyond the ability to cope, He takes over.

**Ruth Bell Graham**

In all your deeds and words, you should look on Jesus as your model, whether you are keeping silence or speaking, whether you are alone or with others.

**St. Bonaventure**

## A Mother-Daughter Prayer

*Dear Lord, we thank You for Your Son. Jesus is the best friend our world has ever known. And, Jesus is our friend and Savior, too. So, we will study Your Word, Lord, and follow in the footsteps of Your Son, now and always. Amen*

# It's Important to Be Kind

*I tell you the truth, anything you did for even the least of my people here, you also did for me.*

**Matthew 25:40 NCV**

The Bible promises that if you're a nice person, good things will happen to you. That's one reason (but not the only reason) that it's important to be kind.

Do you listen to your heart when it tells you to be kind to other people? Hopefully, you do. After all, lots of people in the world aren't as fortunate as you are—and some of these folks are living very near you.

Ask your parents to help you find ways to do nice things for other people. And don't forget that everybody needs love, kindness, and respect, so you should always be ready to share those things, too.

## A Timely Tip for Girls

Kindness should be part of our lives every day, not just on the days when we feel good. Don't try to be kind some of the time, and don't try to be kind to some of the people you know. Instead, try to be kind all of the time, and try to be kind to all the people you know.

# More from God's Word

*Just as you want others to do for you, do the same for them.*

**Luke 6:31 HCSB**

*Finally, all of you be of one mind, having compassion for one another; love as brothers, be tenderhearted, be courteous.*

**1 Peter 3:8 NKJV**

*Love is patient; love is kind.*

**1 Corinthians 13:4 HCSB**

*Let everyone see that you are gentle and kind. The Lord is coming soon.*

**Philippians 4:5 NCV**

## A Timely Tip for Moms

Wise parents understand that kindness matters, and, for that matter, it matters a lot.

## Some Very Bright Ideas

When you extend hospitality to others, you're not trying to impress people, you're trying to reflect God to them.

**Max Lucado**

Reach out and care for someone who needs the touch of hospitality. The time you spend caring today will be a love gift that will blossom into the fresh joy of God's Spirit in the future.

**Emilie Barnes**

Kindness in this world will do much to help others, not only to come into the light, but also to grow in grace day by day.

**Fanny Crosby**

## A Mother-Daughter Prayer

*Dear Lord, it's always the right time to be kind. Help us be kind today, tomorrow, and every day of our lives. Amen*

# White Lies?

*Doing what is right brings freedom to honest people.*

**Proverbs 11:6 ICB**

Sometimes, people convince themselves that it's okay to tell "little white lies." Sometimes people convince themselves that itsy bitsy lies aren't harmful. But there's a problem: little lies have a way of growing into big ones, and once they grow up, they cause lots of problems.

Remember that lies, no matter what size, are not part of God's plan for our lives, so tell the truth about everything. It's the right thing to do, and besides: when you always tell the truth, you don't have to try and remember what you said!

## A Timely Tip for Girls

Little white lies? Beware! You may think that there's a big difference between "little" lies and king-sized ones. Unfortunately, little white lies have a tendency to grow into big trouble . . . in a hurry.

## More from God's Word

*How happy are those whose way is blameless, who live according to the law of the Lord! Happy are those who keep His decrees and seek Him with all their heart.*

**Psalm 119:1-2 HCSB**

*Therefore laying aside falsehood, speak truth, each one of you, with his neighbor, for we are members of one another.*

**Ephesians 4:25 NASB**

*But when he, the Spirit of truth, comes, he will guide you into all truth....*

**John 16:13 NIV**

## A Timely Tip for Moms

Teach the importance of honesty every day, and, if necessary, use words.

# Some Very Bright Ideas

The single most important element in any human relationship is honesty—with oneself, with God, and with others.

**Catherine Marshall**

We must learn, then, to relate transparently and genuinely to others because that is God's style of relating to us.

**Rebecca Manley Pippert**

When you and I are related to Jesus Christ, our strength and wisdom and peace and joy and love and hope may run out, but His life rushes in to keep us filled to the brim. We are showered with blessings, not because of anything we have or have not done, but simply because of Him.

**Anne Graham Lotz**

## A Mother-Daughter Prayer

*Dear Lord, we want to be people whose words are true and whose hearts are pure. In everything that we do, let us use Jesus as our model and our guide. Amen*

# Nobody Likes 'Em

*Therefore, if anyone is in Christ, he is a new creation; the old has gone, the new has come!*

**2 Corinthians 5:17 NIV**

**M**istakes: nobody likes 'em but everybody makes 'em. And you're no different! When you make mistakes (and you will), you should do your best to correct them, to learn from them, and pray for the wisdom to avoid those same mistakes in the future.

If you want to become smarter faster, you'll learn from your mistakes the first time you make them. When you do, that means that you won't keep making the same mistakes over and over again, and that's the smart way to live.

## A Timely Tip for Girls

Made a mistake? Ask for forgiveness! If you've broken one of God's rules, you can always ask Him for His forgiveness. And He will always give it!

# More from God's Word

*If you hide your sins, you will not succeed. If you confess and reject them, you will receive mercy.*

**Proverbs 28:13 NCV**

*If you listen to constructive criticism, you will be at home among the wise.*

**Proverbs 15:31 NLT**

*If we confess our sins to him, he is faithful and just to forgive us and to cleanse us from every wrong.*

**1 John 1:9 NLT**

# A Timely Tip for Moms

Parents make mistakes, too. When you are wrong, admit it. When you do, your children will learn that it's far better to fix problems than to ignore them.

## Some Very Bright Ideas

If at first you don't succeed, read the Instruction Manual—God's.

**Anonymous**

Mistakes offer the possibility for redemption and a new start in God's kingdom. No matter what you're guilty of, God can restore your innocence.

**Barbara Johnson**

When we focus on God, the scene changes. He's in control of our lives; nothing lies outside the realm of His redemptive grace. Even when we make mistakes, fail in relationships, or deliberately make bad choices, God can redeem us.

**Penelope J. Stokes**

## A Mother-Daughter Prayer

*Dear Lord, sometimes we make mistakes. When we do, forgive us, Father. And help us learn from our mistakes so that we can be better people and better examples to our friends and family. Amen*

# Parents Can Help

*The one who lives with integrity is righteous; his children who come after him will be happy.*

**Proverbs 20:7 HCSB**

Whenever you want to get better at something, you should always be willing to let your parents help out in any way they can. After all, your parents want you to become the very best person you can be. So, if you want to become better at controlling your own behavior, ask your parents to help. How can they help out? By reminding you to slow down and think about things before you do them—not after. It's as simple as that.

## A Timely Tip for Girls

Your parents love you and want to help you. Their job is to help . . . your job is to listen carefully to the things they say.

## More from God's Word

*Listen, my son, to your father's instruction and do not forsake your mother's teaching.*

**Proverbs 1:8 NIV**

*Let them first learn to do their duty to their own family and to repay their parents or grandparents. That pleases God.*

**1 Timothy 5:4 NCV**

*Anyone who robs father and mother and says, "So, what's wrong with that?" is worse than a pirate.*

**Proverbs 28:24 MSG**

## A Timely Tip for Moms

Be consistent. Of course there will be times when you feel anger toward your children, but your love for them should never be in question. Parental love must never be turned on and off like the garden hose; it should, instead, flow like a mighty river, too deep to touch bottom and too strong to stop.

## Some Very Bright Ideas

The Bible calls for discipline and a recognition of authority. Children must learn this at home.

**Billy Graham**

God didn't assign the spiritual upbringing of children to churches or Christian schools. He assigned it to parents.

**Beth Moore**

A home is a place where we find direction.

**Gigi Graham Tchividjian**

## A Mother-Daughter Prayer

*Dear God, give us the courage to help others when they need it and the wisdom to accept help when we need it. Amen*

# Your Family Is a Gift

*Love must be without hypocrisy. Detest evil; cling to what is good. Show family affection to one another with brotherly love. Outdo one another in showing honor.*

**Romans 12:9–10 HCSB**

**Y**our family is a wonderful, one-of-a-kind gift from God. And your family members love you very much—what a blessing it is to be loved!

Have you ever really stopped to think about how much you are loved? Your parents love you (of course) and so does everybody else in your family. But it doesn't stop there. You're also an important part of God's family . . . and He loves you more than you can imagine.

What should you do about all the love that comes your way? You should accept it; you should be thankful for it; and you should share it . . . starting now!

## A Timely Tip for Girls

Show and tell: It's good to tell your loved ones how you feel about them, but that's not enough. You should also show them how you feel with your good deeds and your kind words.

# More from God's Word

*If I speak the languages of men and of angels, but do not have love, I am a sounding gong or a clanging cymbal.*

**1 Corinthians 13:1 HCSB**

*Now these three remain: faith, hope, and love. But the greatest of these is love.*

**1 Corinthians 13:13 HCSB**

*Dear friends, if God loved us in this way, we also must love one another.*

**1 John 4:11 HCSB**

# A Timely Tip for Moms

Be expressive. Your children desperately need to hear that you love them . . . from you! If you're bashful, shy, or naturally uncommunicative, get over it.

## Some Very Bright Ideas

I like to think of my family as a big, beautiful patchwork quilt—each of us so different yet stitched together by love and life experiences.

**Barbara Johnson**

God calls upon the loved not just to love but to be loving. God calls upon the forgiven not just to forgive but to be forgiving.

**Beth Moore**

Forgiveness is the precondition of love.

**Catherine Marshall**

## A Mother-Daughter Prayer

*Dear Lord, You have given us a family that cares for us and loves us. Thank You. We will let our family know that we love them by the things that we say and do. You know that we love our family, Lord. Now it's our turn to show them! Amen*

# You Can't Please Everybody

*My son, if sinners entice you, don't be persuaded.*
**Proverbs 1:10 HCSB**

**A**re you one of those girls who tries to please everybody in sight? If so, you'd better watch out! After all, if you worry too much about pleasing your friends, you may not worry enough about pleasing God.

Whom will you try to please tomorrow: your God or your pals? The answer to that question should be simple. Your first job is to obey God's rules . . . and that means obeying your parents, too!

So don't worry too much about pleasing your friends or neighbors. Try, instead, to please your Heavenly Father and your parents. No exceptions.

## A Timely Tip for Girls

You simply cannot please everybody. So here's what you should do: Try pleasing God and your parents.

## More from God's Word

*Blessed is the man who walks not in the counsel of the ungodly, nor stands in the path of sinners, nor sits in the seat of the scornful; but his delight is in the law of the Lord, and in His law he meditates day and night.*

**Psalm 1:1-2 NKJV**

*Do not be deceived: "Bad company corrupts good morals."*

**1 Corinthians 15:33 HCSB**

*Do not be mismatched with unbelievers. For what partnership is there between righteousness and lawlessness? Or what fellowship does light have with darkness?*

**2 Corinthians 6:14 HCSB**

## A Timely Tip for Moms

A great way to guard your steps is by associating with friends who guard theirs.

## Some Very Bright Ideas

If you choose to awaken a passion for God, you will have to choose your friends wisely.

**Lisa Bevere**

It is comfortable to know that we are responsible to God and not to man. It is a small matter to be judged of man's judgement.

**Lottie Moon**

For better or worse, you will eventually become more and more like the people you associate with. So why not associate with people who make you better, not worse?

**Marie T. Freeman**

## A Mother-Daughter Prayer

*Dear Lord, the Bible teaches us that pleasing people is not nearly as important as pleasing You. Let us please You, Lord, today and always. Amen*

# Practicing Forgiveness

*Smart people know how to hold their tongue; their grandeur is to forgive and forget.*

**Proverbs 19:11 MSG**

Forgiving other people requires practice and lots of it. So when it comes to forgiveness, here's something you should remember: if at first you don't succeed, don't give up!

Are you having trouble forgiving someone (or, for that matter, forgiving yourself for a mistake that you've made)? If so, remember that forgiveness isn't easy, so keep trying until you get it right . . . and if you keep trying, you can be sure that sooner or later, you will get it right.

## A Timely Tip for Girls

For most of us—kids and grown-ups alike—forgiveness doesn't come naturally. Keep practicing until it does.

# More from God's Word

*Praise the Lord, I tell myself, and never forget the good things he does for me. He forgives all my sins and heals all my diseases.*

**Psalm 103:3 NLT**

*Therefore, if you are offering your gift at the altar and there remember that your brother has something against you, leave your gift there in front of the alter. First go and be reconciled to your brother, then come and offer your gift.*

**Matthew 5:23-24 NIV**

*And be ye kind one to another, tenderhearted, forgiving one another, even as God for Christ's sake hath forgiven you.*

**Ephesians 4:32 KJV**

## A Timely Tip for Moms

Forgiveness is not optional. God's Word instructs you to forgive others . . . no exceptions.

## Some Very Bright Ideas

As you have received the mercy of God by the forgiveness of sin and the promise of eternal life, thus you must show mercy.

**Billy Graham**

We cannot out-sin God's ability to forgive us.

**Beth Moore**

Only the truly forgiven are truly forgiving.

**C. S. Lewis**

## A Mother-Daughter Prayer

*Dear Lord, please help us forgive other people. You have forgiven us. Now, it's our turn to forgive others. Amen*

# Big Rewards When You Do the Right Thing

*Do you want to be counted wise, to build a reputation for wisdom? Here's what you do: Live well, live wisely, live humbly. It's the way you live, not the way you talk, that counts.*

**James 3:13 MSG**

I f you open up a dictionary, you'll see that the word "wisdom" means "using good judgement, and knowing what is true." But there's more to it than that. It's not enough to know what's right—if you want to be wise, you must also do what's right.

The Bible promises that when you do smart things, you'll earn big rewards, so slow down and think about things before you do them, not after.

## A Timely Tip for Girls

Need wisdom? Listen to your parents, pay attention to God's rules, and choose wise friends.

## More from God's Word

*Teach me, O Lord, the way of Your statutes, and I shall keep it to the end.*

**Psalm 119:33 NKJV**

*So teach us to number our days, that we may gain a heart of wisdom.*

**Psalm 90:12 NKJV**

*Acquire wisdom—how much better it is than gold! And acquire understanding—it is preferable to silver.*

**Proverbs 16:16 HCSB**

## A Timely Tip for Moms

Being a wise parent requires more than knowledge. Knowledge comes from text books, but wisdom comes from God. Wisdom begins with a thorough understanding of God's moral order, the eternal truths that are found in God's Holy Word.

## Some Very Bright Ideas

This is the secret to a lifestyle of worship—doing everything as if you were doing it for Jesus.

**Rick Warren**

Our first step toward gaining God's wisdom is to know what we do not know; that is, to be aware of our shortcomings.

**Dianna Booher**

This is my song through endless ages: Jesus led me all the way.

**Fanny Crosby**

## A Mother-Daughter Prayer

*Dear Lord, let us be patient with other people's mistakes, and let us be patient with our own mistakes. We know that we still have so many things to learn. So we won't stop learning; we won't give up; and we won't stop growing. Amen*

# Be the Right Kind of Christian

*The one who plants and the one who waters have the same purpose, and each will be rewarded for his own work.*

**1 Corinthians 3:8 NCV**

Do want to be the kind of Christian that God intends for you to be? It's up to you! You'll be the one who will decide how you behave.

If you decide to obey God and trust His Son, you will be rewarded now and forever. So guard your heart and trust your Heavenly Father. He will never lead you astray.

## A Timely Tip for Girls

It's easy to blame others when you get into trouble . . . but it's wrong. Instead of trying to blame other people for your own misbehavior, take responsibility . . . and learn from your mistakes!

# More from God's Word

*But each person should examine his own work, and then he will have a reason for boasting in himself alone, and not in respect to someone else. For each person will have to carry his own load.*

**Galatians 6:4-5 HCSB**

*So then each of us shall give account of himself to God.*

**Romans 14:12 NKJV**

*"Therefore I will judge you, O house of Israel, every one according to his ways," says the Lord God.*

**Ezekiel 18:30 NKJV**

# A Timely Tip for Moms

How do parents teach their kids about responsibility? By example, that's how. So if you want to teach the importance of behaving responsibly, remember that demonstrations work better than proclamations.

## Some Very Bright Ideas

Every word we speak, every action we take, has an effect on the totality of humanity. No one can escape that privilege—or that responsibility.

**Laurie Beth Jones**

Although God causes all things to work together for good for His children, He still holds us accountable for our behavior.

**Kay Arthur**

Help yourself and God will help you.

**St. Joan of Arc**

## A Mother-Daughter Prayer

*Dear Lord, thank You for watching over me. Help us understand what's right and do what's right, now and always. Amen*

## Devo 41

# Love Yourself, Too!

*God began doing a good work in you, and I am sure he will continue it until it is finished when Jesus Christ comes again.*

**Philippians 1:6 NCV**

The Bible teaches you this lesson: you should love everybody—and the word "everybody" includes yourself. Do you treat yourself with honor and respect? You should. After all, God created you in a very special way, and He loves you very much. And if God thinks you are amazing and wonderful, shouldn't you think about yourself in the same way? Of course you should!

So remember this: God wants you to love everybody, including the person you see when you look in the mirror. And one more thing: when you learn how to respect the person in the mirror, you'll be better at respecting other people, too.

## A Timely Tip for Girls

When you learn about the Bible, you'll learn how much God loves you.

## More from God's Word

*For you made us only a little lower than God, and you crowned us with glory and honor.*

**Psalm 8:5 NLT**

*How happy are those whose way is blameless, who live according to the law of the Lord! Happy are those who keep His decrees and seek Him with all their heart.*

**Psalm 119:1-2 HCSB**

*Happy is the one whose help is the God of Jacob, whose hope is in the Lord his God.*

**Psalm 146:5 HCSB**

## A Timely Tip for Moms

Your family's collective self-esteem starts at the head of the household and works its way down from there. It's not enough to concern yourself with your child's self-image; you should also strive to become comfortable with your own self-image, too.

## Some Very Bright Ideas

He created us because He delights in us!

**Beth Moore**

Live today fully, expressing gratitude for all you have been, all you are right now, and all you are becoming.

**Melodie Beattie**

May God help us to express and define ourselves in our one-of-a-kind way.

**Luci Swindoll**

## A Mother-Daughter Prayer

*Dear Lord, we have so much to learn and so many ways to improve ourselves. But You love us just as we are. Thank You, Father, for Your love and for Your Son. Amen*

# Learning How to Share

*He that giveth, let him do it with simplicity....*

**Romans 12:8 KJV**

If you're having a little trouble learning how to share your stuff, you're not alone! Most people have problems letting go of things, so don't be discouraged. Just remember that learning to share requires practice and lots of it. The more you share—and the more you learn how good it feels to share—the sooner you'll be able to please God with the generosity and love that flows from your heart.

## A Timely Tip for Girls

The more you share, the better you'll feel about yourself. So if you want to feel very good about yourself, learn to be a very generous person.

# More from God's Word

*In everything I did, I showed you that by this kind of hard work we must help the weak, remembering the words the Lord Jesus himself said: "It is more blessed to give than to receive."*

**Acts 20:35 NIV**

*He that hath two coats, let him impart to him that hath none; and he that hath meat, let him do likewise.*

**Luke 3:11 KJV**

*The righteous give and don't hold back.*

**Proverbs 21:26 HCSB**

# A Timely Tip for Moms

If your child seems to be having trouble sharing, don't hesitate to talk things over with your youngster. The more you talk about sharing, the more likely your child is to share.

## Some Very Bright Ideas

The mind grows by taking in, but the heart grows by giving out.

**Warren Wiersbe**

Generosity is changing one's focus from self to others.

**John Maxwell**

The test of generosity is not how much you give, but how much you have left.

**Anonymous**

## A Mother-Daughter Prayer

*Dear Lord, there are so many things that we can share. Help us never to forget the importance of sharing our possessions, our prayers, and our love with family members and friends. Amen*

# Do the Right Thing . . . and the Kind Thing

*Let everyone see that you are gentle and kind. The Lord is coming soon.*

**Philippians 4:5 NCV**

Sometimes, it's so much easier to do the wrong thing than it is to do the right thing, especially when we're tired or frustrated. But, doing the wrong thing almost always leads to trouble. And sometimes, it leads to BIG trouble.

When you do the right thing, you don't have to worry about what you did or what you said. But, when you do the wrong thing, you'll be worried that someone will find out. So do the right thing, which, by the way, also happens to be the kind thing. You'll be glad you did, and so will other people!

## A Timely Tip for Girls

Kind is as kind does: In order to be a kind person, you must do kind things. Thinking about them isn't enough. So get busy! Your family and friends need all the kindness they can get!

## More from God's Word

*Talk and act like a person expecting to be judged by the Rule that sets us free. For if you refuse to act kindly, you can hardly expect to be treated kindly. Kind mercy wins over harsh judgment every time.*

**James 2:12-13 MSG**

*And may the Lord make you increase and abound in love to one another and to all.*

**1 Thessalonians 3:12 NKJV**

*Love is patient; love is kind.*

**1 Corinthians 13:4 HCSB**

## A Timely Tip for Moms

Kindness is contagious; kids can catch it from their parents.

## Some Very Bright Ideas

When you launch an act of kindness out into the crosswinds of life, it will blow kindness back to you.

**Dennis Swanberg**

If we're to love people like we should, our hearts have to be as pleasant toward them as our appearances are. Otherwise, we're living a lie.

**Mary Hunt**

No one heals himself by wounding another.

**St. Ambrose**

## A Mother-Daughter Prayer

*Dear Lord, we know that You want us to be kind. Help us be kind today, tomorrow, and every day after that. Amen*

# Sharing Is Better Than Being Stingy

*And God will generously provide all you need. Then you will always have everything you need and plenty left over to share with others.*

**2 Corinthians 9:8 NLT**

The Bible teaches that it's better to be generous than selfish. But sometimes, you won't feel like sharing your things, and you'll be tempted to keep everything for yourself. When you're feeling a little bit stingy, remember this: God wants you to share your things, and He will reward you when you do so.

When you learn to be a more generous person, God will be pleased with you . . . and you'll be pleased with yourself. So do yourself (and everybody else) a favor: be a little more generous, starting NOW!

## A Timely Tip for Girls

When you are generous with others, God blesses you even more.

# More from God's Word

*Dear friend, you are showing your faith by whatever you do for the brothers, and this you are doing for strangers.*

**3 John 1:5 HCSB**

*In every way I've shown you that by laboring like this, it is necessary to help the weak and to keep in mind the words of the Lord Jesus, for He said, "It is more blessed to give than to receive."*

**Acts 20:35 HCSB**

*Bear one another's burdens, and so fulfill the law of Christ.*

**Galatians 6:2 NKJV**

## A Timely Tip for Moms

Being kind is a learned behavior. You're the teacher. Class is in session. Your child is in attendance. Actions speak louder than words. And it's one of the most important courses you will ever teach.

## Some Very Bright Ideas

How can we withhold from another what God has so generously allowed us to use and enjoy?

**Jan Winebrenner**

The world says, the more you take, the more you have. Christ says, the more you give, the more you are.

**Frederick Buechner**

Generosity is changing one's focus from self to others.

**John Maxwell**

## A Mother-Daughter Prayer

*Dear Lord, Your Son Jesus was never selfish. Let us follow in His footsteps by sharing with those who need our help. Amen*

# About Barnabas

*Barnabas was a good man, full of the Holy Spirit and full of faith.*

**Acts 11:23-24 ICB**

Barnabas was a leader in the early Christian church who was known for his kindness and for his ability to encourage others. Because of Barnabas, many people were introduced to Christ.

We become like Barnabas when we speak kind words to our families and to our friends. And then, because we have been generous and kind, the people around us can see how Christians should behave. So when in doubt, be kind and generous to others, just like Barnabas.

## A Timely Tip for Girls

Be an encourager! Barnabas was known as a man who encouraged others. In other words, he made other people feel better by saying kind things. You, like Barnabas, can encourage your family and friends . . . and you should.

## More from God's Word

*I want their hearts to be encouraged and joined together in love, so that they may have all the riches of assured understanding, and have the knowledge of God's mystery—Christ.*

**Colossians 2:2 HCSB**

*And let us be concerned about one another in order to promote love and good works.*

**Hebrews 10:24 HCSB**

*Carry one another's burdens; in this way you will fulfill the law of Christ.*

**Galatians 6:2 HCSB**

## A Timely Tip for Moms

Make encouragement a habit. Deliberately look for ways to encourage and praise your children seven days a week. Good deeds and good words can become habit-forming.

# Some Very Bright Ideas

A hug is the ideal gift . . . one size fits all.

**Anonymous**

We do have the ability to encourage or discourage each other with the words we say. In order to maintain a positive mood, our hearts must be in good condition.

**Annie Chapman**

As you're rushing through life, take time to stop a moment, look into people's eyes, say something kind, and try to make them laugh!

**Barbara Johnson**

## A Mother-Daughter Prayer

*Dear Lord, we want to make our family and friends feel better. Please let us say the right words and do the right things now and always. Amen*

# Peace at Home

*My dear brothers, always be willing to listen and slow to speak. Do not become angry easily. Anger will not help you live a good life as God wants.*

**James 1:19 ICB**

Sometimes, it's easy to become angry with the people we love most, and sometimes it's hard to forgive them. After all, we know that our family will still love us no matter how angry we become. But while it's easy to become angry at home, it's usually wrong.

The next time you're tempted to stay angry at a brother, or a sister, or a parent, remember that these are the people who love you more than anybody else! Then, calm down, and forgive them . . . NOW! Because peace is always beautiful, especially when it's peace at your house.

## A Timely Tip for Girls

If you're mad at someone, don't say the first thing that comes to your mind and don't strike out in anger. Instead, catch your breath and start counting until you are once again in control of your temper. If you get to a million and you're still counting, go to bed! You'll feel better in the morning.

# More from God's Word

*When you are angry, do not sin, and be sure to stop being angry before the end of the day. Do not give the devil a way to defeat you.*

**Ephesians 4:26–27 NCV**

*Everyone should be quick to listen, slow to speak and slow to become angry, for man's anger does not bring about the righteous life that God desires.*

**James 1:19-20 NIV**

*God's servant must not be argumentative, but a gentle listener and a teacher who keeps cool, working firmly but patiently with those who refuse to obey. You never know how or when God might sober them up with a change of heart and a turning to the truth.*

**2 Timothy 2:24-25 MSG**

## A Timely Tip for Moms

The way that you manage your own anger will speak volumes to your children. If you can control your anger, you'll help them see the wisdom in controlling theirs.

## Some Very Bright Ideas

When you strike out in anger, you may miss the other person, but you will always hit yourself.

**Jim Gallery**

Anger unresolved will only bring you woe.

**Kay Arthur**

Bitterness and anger, usually over trivial things, make havoc of homes, churches, and friendships.

**Warren Wiersbe**

You don't have to attend every argument you're invited to!

**Anonymous**

## A Mother-Daughter Prayer

*Dear Lord, if we become angry with family or friends, calm us down. Jesus forgave everybody, even the people who hurt Him. We should, too. Amen*

# The Blame Game

*People's own foolishness ruins their lives, but in their minds they blame the Lord.*

**Proverbs 19:3 NCV**

**W**hen something goes wrong, do you look for somebody to blame? And do you try to blame other people even if you're the one who made the mistake? Hopefully not!

It's silly to try to blame other people for your own mistakes, so don't do it.

If you've done something you're ashamed of, don't look for somebody to blame; look for a way to say, "I'm sorry, and I won't make that same mistake again."

## A Timely Tip for Girls

It's very tempting to blame others when you make a mistake, but it's more honest to look in the mirror first.

# More from God's Word

*Get rid of all bitterness, rage, anger, harsh words, and slander, as well as all types of malicious behavior. Instead, be kind to each other, tenderhearted, forgiving one another, just as God through Christ has forgiven you.*

**Ephesians 4:31–32 NLT**

*Don't insist on getting even; that's not for you to do. "I'll do the judging," says God. "I'll take care of it."*

**Romans 12:19 MSG**

*See to it that no one repays evil for evil to anyone, but always pursue what is good for one another and for all.*

**1 Thessalonians 5:15 HCSB**

# A Timely Tip for Moms

The blame game has no winners. So don't allow your child to play it.

## Some Very Bright Ideas

Instead of looking for someone to blame, look for something to fix, and then get busy fixing it.

**Criswell Freeman**

Replace your excuses with fresh determination.

**Charles Swindoll**

You'll never win the blame game, so why even bother to play?

**Anonymous**

## A Mother-Daughter Prayer

*Dear Lord, when we make mistakes, it's tempting to blame others. But blaming others is wrong. Help us accept responsibility, Father, for the mistakes we make. And help us learn from them. Amen*

**Devo 48**

# What Your Conscience Says About Forgiveness

*Now the goal of our instruction is love from a pure heart, a good conscience, and a sincere faith.*

**1 Timothy 1:5 HCSB**

God gave you something called a conscience: it's that little feeling that tells you whether something is right or wrong. Your conscience will usually tell you what to do and when to do it. Trust that feeling.

If you listen to your conscience, it won't be as hard for you to forgive people. Why? Because forgiving other people is the right thing to do. And, it's what God wants you to do. And it's what your conscience tells you to do. So what are you waiting for?

## A Timely Tip for Girls

Trust the quiet inner voice of your conscience: Treat your conscience as you would a trusted advisor.

# More from God's Word

*So I strive always to keep my conscience clear before God and man.*

**Acts 24:16 NIV**

*If then you were raised with Christ, seek those things which are above, where Christ is, sitting at the right hand of God. Set your mind on things above, not on things on the earth.*

**Colossians 3:1-2 NKJV**

*Let us come near to God with a sincere heart and a sure faith, because we have been made free from a guilty conscience, and our bodies have been washed with pure water.*

**Hebrews 10:22 NCV**

# A Timely Tip for Moms

That quiet little voice inside your head will guide you down the right path if you listen carefully. Very often, your conscience will actually tell you what God wants you to do. So listen, learn, and behave accordingly.

## Some Very Bright Ideas

Nobody is good by accident.

**C. H. Spurgeon**

Obedience is the outward expression of your love of God.

**Henry Blackaby**

Although God causes all things to work together for good for His children, He still holds us accountable for our behavior.

**Kay Arthur**

## A Mother-Daughter Prayer

*Dear Lord, we know that we should forgive other people. So when it's time to forgive, that's exactly what we'll do. Amen*

# Jesus Offers Peace

*I have told you these things, so that in me you may have peace. In this world you will have trouble. But take heart! I have overcome the world.*

**John 16:33 NIV**

Jesus offers us peace . . . peace in our hearts and peace in our homes. But He doesn't force us to enjoy His peace—we can either accept His peace or not.

When we accept the peace of Jesus Christ by opening up our hearts to Him, we feel much better about ourselves, our families, and our lives.

Would you like to feel a little better about yourself and a little better about your corner of the world? Then open up your heart to Jesus, because that's where real peace begins.

## A Timely Tip for Girls

You have a big role to play in helping to maintain a peaceful home. It's a big job, so don't be afraid to ask for help . . . especially God's help.

## More from God's Word

*God has called us to peace.*

**1 Corinthians 7:15 NKJV**

*Be of good comfort, be of one mind, live in peace; and the God of love and peace will be with you.*

**2 Corinthians 13:11 NKJV**

*For He is our peace.*

**Ephesians 2:14 HCSB**

## A Timely Tip for Moms

God offers peace that passes human understanding . . . and He wants you to make His peace your peace.

## Some Very Bright Ideas

A great many people are trying to make peace, but that has already been done. God has not left it for us to do; all we have to do is to enter into it.

**D. L. Moody**

Where the soul is full of peace and joy, outward surroundings and circumstances are of comparatively little account.

**Hannah Whitall Smiith**

Peace with God is where all peace begins.

**Jim Gallery**

## A Mother-Daughter Prayer

*Dear Lord, we thank You for our family. Help us treat our family members with love and respect, today every day. Amen*

# Positive Peer Pressure

*My dear, dear friends, if God loved us like this, we certainly ought to love each other.*

**1 John 4:11 MSG**

Are your friends the kind of kids who encourage you to behave yourself? If so, you've chosen your friends wisely.

But if your friends try to get you in trouble, perhaps it's time to think long and hard about making some new friends.

Whether you know it or not, you're probably going to behave like your friends behave. So pick out friends who make you want to behave better, not worse. When you do, you'll be saving yourself from a lot of trouble . . . a whole lot of trouble.

## A Timely Tip for Girls

Choose wise friends, and listen carefully to the things they say.

# More from God's Word

*Do not be misled: "Bad company corrupts good character."*

**1 Corinthians 15:33 NIV**

*For am I now trying to win the favor of people, or God? Or am I striving to please people? If I were still trying to please people, I would not be a slave of Christ.*

**Galatians 1:10 HCSB**

*Stay away from a foolish man; you will gain no knowledge from his speech.*

**Proverbs 14:7 HCSB**

# A Timely Tip for Moms

Do you want your child to choose well-behaved friends? If so, talk openly to your child about the wisdom of choosing friends who behave themselves.

## Some Very Bright Ideas

You can make more friends in two months by becoming more interested in other people than you can in two years by trying to get other people interested in you.

**Dale Carnegie**

My special friends, who know me so well and love me anyway, give me daily encouragement to keep on.

**Emilie Barnes**

God has not called us to see through each other, but to see each other through.

**Jess Moody**

## A Mother-Daughter Prayer

*Dear Lord, the Bible teaches us to choose our friends carefully. And, that's what we intend to do every day of our lives. Amen*

# How Do They Know?

*Do you want to be counted wise, to build a reputation for wisdom? Here's what you do: Live well, live wisely, live humbly. It's the way you live, not the way you talk, that counts.*

**James 3:13 MSG**

How do people know that you're a Christian? Well, you can tell them, of course. And make no mistake about it: talking about your faith in God is a very good thing to do. But simply telling people about Jesus isn't enough. You must also be willing to show people how a real Christian (like you) should behave. Does that sound like a big responsibility? It is . . . but you can do it!

## A Timely Tip for Girls

The life you live is your most important testimony.

## More from God's Word

*Do everything without grumbling and arguing, so that you may be blameless and pure.*

**Philippians 2:14–15 HCSB**

*Set an example of good works yourself, with integrity and dignity in your teaching.*

**Titus 2:7 HCSB**

*For the kingdom of God is not in talk but in power.*

**1 Corinthians 4:20 HCSB**

## A Timely Tip for Moms

Give your children the gift of a lifetime. How? By being a worthy example.

## Some Very Bright Ideas

Actions speak louder than words; let your words teach and your actions speak.

**St. Anthony of Padua**

Living life with a consistent spiritual walk deeply influences those we love most.

**Vonette Bright**

We have in Jesus Christ a perfect example of how to put God's truth into practice.

**Bill Bright**

## A Mother-Daughter Prayer

*Dear Lord, help us follow in the footsteps of Your Son so that we can show other people what it really means to be a Christian. Amen*

# Choosing Wisely

*I am offering you life or death, blessings or curses. Now, choose life! . . . To choose life is to love the Lord your God, obey him, and stay close to him.*

**Deuteronomy 30:19-20 NCV**

Choices, choices, choices! You've got so many choices to make, and sometimes, making those choices isn't easy. At times you're torn between what you want to do and what you ought to do. When that happens, it's up to you to choose wisely . . . or else!

When you make wise choices, you are rewarded; when you make unwise choices, you must accept the consequences. It's as simple as that. So make sure that your choices are pleasing to God . . . or else!

## A Timely Tip for Girls

Wise choices bring you happiness; unwise choices don't. So whenever you have a choice to make, choose wisely.

# More from God's Word

*The thing you should want most is God's kingdom and doing what God wants. Then all these other things you need will be given to you.*

**Matthew 6:33 NCV**

*If you don't know what you're doing, pray to the Father. He loves to help. You'll get his help, and won't be condescended to when you ask for it. Ask boldly, believingly, without a second thought. People who "worry their prayers" are like wind-whipped waves. Don't think you're going to get anything from the Master that way, adrift at sea, keeping all your options open.*

**James 1:5-8 MSG**

## A Timely Tip for Moms

Of course you want to give your children room to grow, but some decisions must be reserved for the wisest, most mature men and women of the family (moms and dads). Big decisions, especially decisions about health and safety, should be made by thoughtful parents, not children.

## Some Very Bright Ideas

Freedom is not the right to do what we want but the power to do what we ought.

**Corrie ten Boom**

Every step of your life's journey is a choice . . . and the quality of those choices determines the quality of the journey.

**Criswell Freeman**

Faith is not a feeling; it is action. It is a willed choice.

**Elisabeth Elliot**

## A Mother-Daughter Prayer

*Dear God, we have many choices to make. Help us choose wisely as we follow in the footsteps of Your Son. Amen*

# Your Attitude

*Make your own attitude that of Christ Jesus.*

**Philippians 2:5 HCSB**

What's an attitude? The word "attitude" means "the way that you think." And don't forget this: your attitude is important.

Your attitude can make you happy or sad, grumpy or glad, joyful or mad. And, your attitude doesn't just control the way that you think; it also controls how you behave. If you have a good attitude, you'll behave well. And if you have a bad attitude, you're more likely to misbehave.

Have you spent any time thinking about the way that you think? Do you pay much attention to your attitude? Hopefully so! After all, a good attitude is better than a bad one . . . lots better.

You have more control over your attitude than you think. So do your best to make your attitude a good attitude. One way you can do that is by learning about Jesus and about His attitude toward life. When you do, you'll learn that it's always better to think good thoughts, and it's always better to do good things. Always!

## A Timely Tip for Girls

What will you pay attention to tomorrow? Try to pay careful attention to God's blessings, to God's love, and to God's rules. When you do, you'll be happier.

## More from God's Word

*Finally brothers, whatever is true, whatever is honorable, whatever is just, whatever is pure, whatever is lovely, whatever is commendable—if there is any moral excellence and if there is any praise—dwell on these things.*

**Philippians 4:8 HCSB**

*For the word of God is living and powerful, and sharper than any two-edged sword, piercing even to the division of soul and spirit, and of joints and marrow, and is a discerner of the thoughts and intents of the heart.*

**Hebrews 4:12 NKJV**

## A Timely Tip for Moms

Where is your focus today? Remember that it's important to focus your thoughts on the positive aspects of life, not the negative ones.

## Some Very Bright Ideas

Attitude is the mind's paintbrush; it can color any situation.

**Barbara Johnson**

Life is 10% what happens to you and 90% how you respond to it.

**Charles Swindoll**

Each one of us is responsible for our own happiness. If we choose to allow ourselves to become miserable and unhappy, the problem is ours, not someone else's.

**Joyce Meyer**

## A Mother-Daughter Prayer

*Dear Lord, help us have an attitude that is pleasing to You. And, let us remember to count our blessings today, tomorrow, and every day after that. Amen*

# Celebrate!

*Celebrate God all day, every day. I mean, revel in him!*

**Philippians 4:4 MSG**

D o you feel like celebrating? Hopefully so! Are you expecting God to do wonderful things? Hopefully so! Are you happy about your family, your friends, and your church? Hopefully so! After all, God loves you, and that fact should make you very happy indeed. So treat every day as a big celebration . . . because that's exactly what every day should be.

## A Timely Tip for Girls

Every day is a cause for celebration: Psalm 118:24 has clear instructions for the coming day: "This is the day which the LORD has made; let us rejoice and be glad in it." Plan your day—and your life—accordingly.

# More from God's Word

*I will praise you, Lord, with all my heart. I will tell all the miracles you have done. I will be happy because of you; God Most High, I will sing praises to your name.*

**Psalm 9:1-2 NCV**

*A joyful heart is good medicine, but a broken spirit dries up the bones.*

**Proverbs 17:22 HCSB**

*How happy is the man who does not follow the advice of the wicked, or take the path of sinners, or join a group of mockers!*

**Psalm 1:1 HCSB**

## A Timely Tip for Moms

God has given you the gift of life (here on earth) and the promise of eternal life (in heaven). Now, He wants you to celebrate those gifts and share your joy with your family.

## Some Very Bright Ideas

The highest and most desirable state of the soul is to praise God in celebration for being alive.

**Luci Swindol**

If you can forgive the person you were, accept the person you are, and believe in the person you will become, you are headed for joy. So celebrate your life.

**Barbara Johnson**

Not every day of our lives is overflowing with joy and celebration. But there are moments when our hearts nearly burst within us for the sheer joy of being alive. The first sight of our newborn babies, the warmth of love in another's eyes, the fresh scent of rain on a hot summer's eve—moments like these renew in us a heartfelt appreciation for life.

**Gwen Ellis**

## A Mother-Daughter Prayer

*Dear Lord, help us remember that every day is a cause for celebration. Today, we will keep joy in our hearts as we celebrate Your blessings and Your Son. Amen*

# Be Happy Today

*But happy are those . . . whose hope is in the LORD their God.*

**Psalm 146:5 NLT**

I f we could decide to be happy "once and for all," life would be so much simpler, but it doesn't seem to work that way. If we want happiness to last, we need to create good thoughts every day that we live. Yesterday's good thoughts don't count . . . we've got to think more good thoughts now.

Each new day is a gift from God, so treat it that way. Think about it like this: today is another wonderful chance to celebrate God's gifts.

So celebrate—starting now—and keep celebrating forever!

## A Timely Tip for Girls

Better self-control can help make you happy: the better you behave, the more fun you'll have. And don't let anybody try to tell you otherwise.

## More from God's Word

*But the truly happy person is the one who carefully studies God's perfect law that makes people free. He continues to study it. He listens to God's teaching and does not forget what he heard. Then he obeys what God's teaching says. When he does this, it makes him happy.*

**James 1:25 ICB**

*Happy are those who fear the Lord. Yes, happy are those who delight in doing what he commands.*

**Psalm 112:1 NLT**

*Delight thyself also in the LORD; and he shall give thee the desires of thine heart.*

**Psalm 37:4 KJV**

## A Timely Tip for Moms

Your children deserve to grow up in a happy home. As a parent, you owe it to them (and to yourself) to provide that kind of home.

## Some Very Bright Ideas

When the dream of our heart is one that God has planted there, a strange happiness flows into us. At that moment, all of the spiritual resources of the universe are released to help us. Our praying is then at one with the will of God and becomes a channel for the Creator's purposes for us and our world.

**Catherine Marshall**

Those who are God's without reserve are, in every sense, content.

**Hannah Whitall Smith**

No matter how hard he searches, nothing beneath the skies and nothing above the skies can make any man happy apart from God.

**C. H. Spurgeon**

## A Mother-Daughter Prayer

*Dear Lord, You have given us so many reasons to be happy. Every day, we will try to be joyful Christians as we give thanks for Your gifts, for Your love, and for Your Son. Amen*

# Setting an Example

*Set an example of good works yourself, with integrity and dignity in your teaching.*

**Titus 2:7 HCSB**

The Bible says that you are "the light that gives light to the world." The Bible also says that you should live in a way that lets other people understand what it means to be a good person. And of course, learning to share is an important part of being a good person.

What kind of "light" have you been giving off? Hopefully, you have been a good example for everybody to see. Why? Because the world needs all the light it can get, and that includes your light, too!

## A Timely Tip for Girls

Think about the ways that your behavior impacts your family and friends.

# More from God's Word

*For the kingdom of God is not in talk but in power.*

**1 Corinthians 4:20 HCSB**

*Therefore since we also have such a large cloud of witnesses surrounding us, let us lay aside every weight and the sin that so easily ensnares us, and run with endurance the race that lies before us.*

**Hebrews 12:1 HCSB**

*Test all things; hold fast what is good. Abstain from every form of evil.*

**1 Thessalonians 5:21-22 NKJV**

# A Timely Tip for Moms

Parental pronouncements are easy to make but much harder to live by. But whether you like it or not, you are almost certainly the most important role model for your child. Behave accordingly.

## Some Very Bright Ideas

Your life is destined to be an example. The only question is "what kind?"

**Marie T. Freeman**

One of the best ways to witness to family, friends, and neighbors is to let them see the difference Jesus has made in your life.

**Anne Graham Lotz**

It's good to be saved and know it! It's also good to be saved and show it!

**Anonymous**

## A Mother-Daughter Prayer

*Dear Lord, let our lights shine brightly for You. Let us be positive examples for all to see, and let us share love and kindness with our family and friends. Amen*

# Feeling Better

*A wise person is patient. He will be honored if he ignores a wrong done against him.*

**Proverbs 19:11 ICB**

Is forgiving someone else an easy thing for you to do or a hard thing? If you're like most people, forgiving others can be hard, Hard, HARD! But even if you're having a very hard time forgiving someone, you can do it if you talk things over with your parents, and if you talk things over with God.

Do you find forgiveness difficult? Talk about it and pray about it. You'll feel better when you do.

## A Timely Tip for Girls

How hard is it to love your enemies? You'll never know until you try . . . so try!

## More from God's Word

*Our Father is kind; you be kind. "Don't pick on people, jump on their failures, criticize their faults—unless, of course, you want the same treatment. Don't condemn those who are down; that hardness can boomerang. Be easy on people; you'll find life a lot easier."*

**Luke 6:36-37 MSG**

*Do not judge, and you will not be judged. Do not condemn, and you will not be condemned. Forgive, and you will be forgiven.*

**Luke 6:37 HCSB**

*And whenever you stand praying, if you have anything against anyone, forgive him, so that your Father in heaven may also forgive you your wrongdoing.*

**Mark 11:25 HCSB**

## A Timely Tip for Moms

Until you learn how to forgive, you're locked inside a prison of your own making.

## Some Very Bright Ideas

When God forgives, He forgets. He buries our sins in the sea and puts a sign on the shore saying, "No Fishing Allowed."

**Corrie ten Boom**

Forgiveness is the precondition of love.

**Catherine Marshall**

Forgiveness is every person's deepest need and the greatest quality of being like Jesus.

**Franklin Graham**

## A Mother-Daughter Prayer

*Dear Lord, even when forgiveness is hard, help us be people who forgive others, just as You have forgiven us. Amen*

# God Is Right Here

*Fear not, for I am with you; Be not dismayed, for I am your God.
I will strengthen you.*

**Isaiah 41:10 NKJV**

Here's a promise you can depend on: Wherever you are, God is always there, too.

God doesn't take vacations, and He doesn't play hide-and-seek. He's always "right here, right now," waiting to hear from you. So if you're wondering where God is, wonder no more. He's here. And that's a promise!

## A Timely Tip for Girls

God's presence provides comfort. Seek Him often and pray often.

# More from God's Word

*No, I will not abandon you as orphans—I will come to you.*

**John 14:18 NLT**

*Again, this is God's command: to believe in his personally named Son, Jesus Christ. He told us to love each other, in line with the original command. As we keep his commands, we live deeply and surely in him, and he lives in us. And this is how we experience his deep and abiding presence in us: by the Spirit he gave us.*

**1 John 3:23-24 MSG**

*You will seek Me and find Me when you search for Me with all your heart.*

**Jeremiah 29:13 HCSB**

## A Timely Tip for Moms

God isn't far away—He's right here, right now. And He's willing to talk to you right here, right now.

## Some Very Bright Ideas

The tender eyes of God perpetually see us. He has never stopped noticing.

**Angela Thomas**

Through the death and broken body of Jesus Christ on the Cross, you and I have been given access to the presence of God when we approach Him by faith in prayer.

**Anne Graham Lotz**

Give yourself a gift today: be present with yourself. God is. Enjoy your own personality. God does.

**Barbara Johnson**

## A Mother-Daughter Prayer

*Dear Lord, You are always with us, and You are always listening to our thoughts and to our prayers. We will pray to You often, and we will trust in You always. Amen*

# Love to Share

*And we have known and believed the love that God has for us. God is love, and he who abides in love abides in God, and God in him.*

**1 John 4:16 NKJV**

The Bible tells us that God is love and that if we wish to know Him, we must have love in our hearts. Sometimes, of course, when we're tired, angry, or frustrated, it is very hard for us to be loving. Thankfully, anger and frustration are feelings that come and go, but God's love lasts forever.

If you'd like to improve your day and your life, share God's love with your family and friends. Every time you love, and every time you give, God smiles.

## A Timely Tip for Girls

God's love is our greatest security blanket: Kay Arthur advises, "Snuggle in God's arms. When you are hurting, when you feel lonely or left out, let Him cradle you, comfort you, reassure you of His all-sufficient power and love." Enough said.

## More from God's Word

*Help me, Lord my God; save me according to Your faithful love.*

**Psalm 109:26 HCSB**

*Whoever is wise will observe these things, and they will understand the lovingkindness of the Lord.*

**Psalm 107:43 NKJV**

*The Lord is gracious and compassionate, slow to anger and great in faithful love. The Lord is good to everyone; His compassion [rests] on all He has made.*

**Psalm 145:8-9 HCSB**

## A Timely Tip for Moms

When all else fails, God's love does not. You can always depend upon God's love . . . and He is always your ultimate protection.

## Some Very Bright Ideas

The Christian life is motivated, not by a list of do's and don'ts, but by the gracious outpouring of God's love and blessing.

**Anne Graham Lotz**

God loves you whether you like it or not.

**Anonymous**

We cannot protect ourselves from trouble, but we can dance through the puddles of life with a rainbow smile, twirling the only umbrella we need—the umbrella of God's love.

**Barbara Johnson**

## A Mother-Daughter Prayer

*Dear Lord, You are the truth and the light. We will make You our truth and our light. Amen*

# Draw a Picture Together about Sharing Your Love

# Patiently Waiting

*We can make our plans, but the LORD determines our steps.*

**Proverbs 16:9 NLT**

God has a plan for you. But God's plan may not always happen in the way that you would like or at the time of your own choosing. Still, God always knows best.

Sometimes, even though you may want something very badly, you must still be patient and wait for the right time to get it. And the right time, of course, is determined by God. So trust Him always, obey Him always, and wait for Him to show you His plans. And that's exactly what He will do.

## A Timely Tip for Girls

God has very big plans in store for your life, so trust Him and wait patiently for those plans to unfold. And remember: God's timing is best.

# More from God's Word

*The Lord says, "I will guide you along the best pathway for your life. I will advise you and watch over you."*

**Psalm 32:8 NLT**

*"I say this because I know what I am planning for you," says the Lord. "I have good plans for you, not plans to hurt you. I will give you hope and a good future."*

**Jeremiah 29:11 NCV**

*We know that all things work together for the good of those who love God: those who are called according to His purpose.*

**Romans 8:28 HCSB**

## A Timely Tip for Moms

God has a wonderful plan for your life. And the time to start looking for that plan—and living it—is now. Discovering God's plan begins with prayer, but it doesn't end there. You've also got to work at it.

## Some Very Bright Ideas

God isn't a talent scout looking for someone who is "good enough" or "strong enough." He is looking for someone with a heart set on Him, and He will do the rest.

**Vance Havner**

God will never lead you where His strength cannot keep you.

**Barbara Johnson**

God wants us to serve Him with a willing spirit, one that would choose no other way.

**Beth Moore**

## A Mother-Daughter Prayer

*Dear Lord, You have wonderful plans for us. Let us discover those plans so that we can become the people You want us to become. Amen*

# **Respecting Others**

*Just as you want others to do for you, do the same for them.*
**Luke 6:31 HCSB**

ow should you treat other people? Jesus has the answer to that question. Jesus wants you to treat other people exactly like you want to be treated: with kindness, respect, and courtesy. When you do, you'll make your family and friends happy . . . and that's what God wants.

So if you're wondering how to treat someone else, follow the Golden Rule: treat the other people like you want them to treat you. When you do, you'll be obeying your Father in heaven and you'll be making other folks happy at the same time.

## **A Timely Tip for Girls**

When dealing with other people, it is important to try to walk in their shoes.

## More from God's Word

*See that no one renders evil for evil to anyone, but always pursue what is good both for yourselves and for all.*

**1 Thessalonians 5:15 NKJV**

*If you really carry out the royal law prescribed in Scripture, You shall love your neighbor as yourself, you are doing well.*

**James 2:8 HCSB**

*And let us not grow weary while doing good, for in due season we shall reap if we do not lose heart.*

**Galatians 6:9 NKJV**

## A Timely Tip for Moms

Kids imitate parents, so act accordingly! The best way for your child to learn the Golden Rule is by example . . . your example!

## Some Very Bright Ideas

It is one of the most beautiful compensations of life that no one can sincerely try to help another without helping herself.

**Barbara Johnson**

The Golden Rule starts at home, but it should never stop there.

**Marie T. Freeman**

The #1 rule of friendship is the Golden one.

**Criswell Freeman**

## A Mother-Daughter Prayer

*Dear Lord, help us always to do our very best to treat others as we wish to be treated. The Golden Rule is Your rule, Father. We will make it our rule, too. Amen*

# Changing Habits

*Do not be deceived: "Evil company corrupts good habits."*
**1 Corinthians 15:33 NKJV**

**M**ost girls have a few habits they'd like to change, and maybe you do, too. If so, God can help.

If you trust God, and if you keep asking Him to help you change bad habits, He will help you make yourself into a new person. So, if at first you don't succeed, keep praying. God is listening, and He's ready to help you become a better person if you ask Him . . . so ask Him!

## A Timely Tip for Girls

The old saying is familiar and true: "First you make your habits; then your habits make you." So it's always a good time to ask this question: "What kind of person are my habits making me?"

# More from God's Word

*Above all else, guard your heart, for it affects everything you do.*
**Proverbs 4:23 NLT**

*The peace of God, which surpasses all understanding, will guard your hearts and minds through Christ Jesus.*
**Philippians 4:7 NKJV**

*Don't copy the behavior and customs of this world, but let God transform you into a new person by changing the way you think. Then you will know what God wants you to do, and you will know how good and pleasing and perfect his will really is.*
**Romans 12:2 NLT**

# A Timely Tip for Moms

Target your most unhealthy habit first, and attack it with vigor. When it comes to defeating harmful habitual behaviors, you'll need focus, determination, prayer, more focus, more determination, and more prayer.

## Some Very Bright Ideas

If you want to form a new habit, get to work. If you want to break a bad habit, get on your knees.

**Marie T. Freeman**

He who does not overcome small faults, shall fall little by little into greater ones.

**Thomas à Kempis**

Begin to be now what you will be hereafter.

**St. Jerome**

## A Mother-Daughter Prayer

*Dear Lord, please help us do things that are pleasing to You, and help us form habits that are pleasing to You. Amen*

# Always Be Honest

*The honest person will live safely, but the one who is dishonest will be caught.*

**Proverbs 10:9 ICB**

**N**obody can tell the truth for you. You're the one who decides what you are going to say. You're the one who decides whether your words will be truthful . . . or not.

The word "integrity" means doing the right and honest thing. If you're going to be a person of integrity, it's up to you. If you want to live a life that is pleasing to God and to others, make integrity a habit. When you do, everybody wins, especially you!

## A Timely Tip for Girls

Unless you build your friendships on honesty, you're building on a slippery slope.

## More from God's Word

*Ye shall not steal, neither deal falsely, neither lie one to another.*

**Leviticus 19:11 KJV**

*The one who lives with integrity lives securely, but whoever perverts his ways will be found out.*

**Proverbs 10:9 HCSB**

*The one who lives with integrity will be helped, but one who distorts right and wrong will suddenly fall.*

**Proverbs 28:18 HCSB**

## A Timely Tip for Moms

Telling the truth isn't just hard for kids; it can be hard for parents, too. And when honesty is hard, that's precisely the moment when wise parents remember that their children are watching . . . and learning.

## Some Very Bright Ideas

One thing that is important for stable emotional health is honesty—with self and with others.

**Joyce Meyer**

Those who are given to white lies soon become color blind.

**Anonymous**

Much guilt arises in the life of the believer from practicing the chameleon life of environmental adaptation.

**Beth Moore**

## A Mother-Daughter Prayer

*Dear Lord, the Bible teaches us that honesty is the best policy. Help us remember the importance of honesty today and every day of our lives. Amen*

# Getting to Know Him

*If your life honors the name of Jesus, he will honor you.*

**2 Thessalonians 1:12 MSG**

There's really no way around it: If you want to know God, you need to know His Son. And that's good, because getting to know Jesus can—and should—be a wonderful experience.

Jesus has an amazing love for you, so welcome Him into your heart today. When you do, you'll always be grateful that you did.

## A Timely Tip for Girls

When it comes to telling the world about your relationship with God, your actions speak much more loudly than your words . . . so behave accordingly.

# More from God's Word

*The next day John saw Jesus coming toward him and said, "Here is the Lamb of God, who takes away the sin of the world!"*
**John 1:29 HCSB**

*I am the door. If anyone enters by Me, he will be saved.*
**John 10:9 NKJV**

*I have come as a light into the world, so that everyone who believes in Me would not remain in darkness.*
**John 12:46 HCSB**

# A Timely Tip for Moms

Jesus loves you, and He offers you eternal life with Him in heaven. Welcome Him into your heart. Now! For your sake and for your children's sake.

## Some Very Bright Ideas

The crucial question for each of us is this: What do you think of Jesus, and do you yet have a personal acquaintance with Him?

**Hannah Whitall Smith**

When we are in a situation where Jesus is all we have, we soon discover he is all we really need.

**Gigi Graham Tchividjian**

If Jesus is the preeminent One in our lives, then we will love each other, submit to each other, and treat one another fairly in the Lord.

**Warren Wiersbe**

## A Mother-Daughter Prayer

*Dear Lord, thank You for Your Son Jesus. Jesus is our friend, and we will try to know Him better this day and every day. Amen*

# Kindness Starts with You

*Be kind to one another, tender-hearted, forgiving each other, just as God in Christ also has forgiven you.*

**Ephesians 4:32 NASB**

If you're waiting for other people to be nice to you before you're nice to them, you've got it backwards. Kindness starts with you! You see, you can never control what other people will say or do, but you can control your own behavior.

The Bible tells us that we should never stop doing good deeds as long as we live. Kindness is God's way, and it should be our way, too.

## A Timely Tip for Girls

In order to be a kind person, you must do kind things. Thinking about them isn't enough. So get busy! Your family and friends need all the kindness they can get!

## More from God's Word

*A kind man benefits himself, but a cruel man brings disaster on himself.*

**Proverbs 11:17 HCSB**

*Love is patient; love is kind.*

**1 Corinthians 13:4 HCSB**

*Therefore, God's chosen ones, holy and loved, put on heartfelt compassion, kindness, humility, gentleness, and patience.*

**Colossians 3:12 HCSB**

## A Timely Tip for Moms

Kindness is contagious; kids can catch it from their parents.

## Some Very Bright Ideas

It doesn't take monumental feats to make the world a better place. It can be as simple as letting someone go ahead of you in a grocery line.

**Barbara Johnson**

Showing kindness to others is one of the nicest things we can do for ourselves.

**Janette Oke**

If I am inconsiderate about the comfort of others, or their feelings, or even their little weaknesses; if I am careless about their little hurts and miss opportunities to smooth their way; if I make the sweet running of household wheels more difficult to accomplish, then I know nothing of Calvary's love.

**Amy Carmichael**

## A Mother-Daughter Prayer

*Dear Lord, sometimes it's easy to be nice to people and sometimes it's not so easy. When it's hard to be kind, Lord, help us say the right things and do the right things. Amen*

# Think Good Thoughts

*Come near to God, and God will come near to you. You sinners, clean sin out of your lives. You who are trying to follow God and the world at the same time, make your thinking pure.*

**James 4:8 NCV**

Do you try to think good thoughts about your friends, your family, and yourself? The Bible says that you should. Do you lift your hopes and your prayers to God many times each day? The Bible says that you should. Do you say "no" to people who want you to do bad things or think bad thoughts? The Bible says that you should.

The Bible teaches you to guard your thoughts against things that are hurtful or wrong. So remember this: When you turn away from bad thoughts and turn instead toward God and His Son Jesus, you will be protected . . . and you will be blessed.

## A Timely Tip for Girls

Good thoughts can lead you to some very good places . . . and bad thoughts can lead elsewhere.

# More from God's Word

*So prepare your minds for service and have self-control.*

**1 Peter 1:13 NCV**

*Those who are pure in their thinking are happy, because they will be with God.*

**Matthew 5:8 NCV**

*And now, dear brothers and sisters, let me say one more thing as I close this letter. Fix your thoughts on what is true and honorable and right. Think about things that are pure and lovely and admirable. Think about things that are excellent and worthy of praise.*

**Philippians 4:8 NLT**

# A Timely Tip for Moms

Believe it or not, your child is probably a mind reader. If your kid is like most kids, she is surprisingly sensitive. So do yourself and your child a favor: be careful with your thoughts as well as your actions.

## Some Very Bright Ideas

Attitude is the mind's paintbrush; it can color any situation.

**Barbara Johnson**

The things we think are the things that feed our souls. If we think on pure and lovely things, we shall grow pure and lovely like them; and the converse is equally true.

**Hannah Whitall Smith**

Preoccupy my thoughts with your praise beginning today.

**Joni Eareckson Tada**

## A Mother-Daughter Prayer

*Dear Lord, help us think good thoughts—and help us do good things—now and always. Amen*

# Perfect Love

*For God so loved the world that he gave his only Son, so that everyone who believes in him will not perish but have eternal life.*

**John 3:16 NLT**

The Bible makes this promise: God is love. It's a big promise, a very important description of what God is and how God works. God's love is perfect. When we open our hearts to His love, we are blessed and we are protected.

Tonight, offer sincere prayers of thanksgiving to your Heavenly Father. He loves you now and throughout all eternity. Open your heart to His presence and His love.

## A Timely Tip for Girls

God loves you more than you can imagine, and He's prepared a place for you in heaven. So celebrate God's love today and every day.

## More from God's Word

*Unfailing love surrounds those who trust the LORD.*

**Psalm 32:10 NLT**

*For the LORD your God has arrived to live among you. He is a mighty savior. He will rejoice over you with great gladness. With his love, he will calm all your fears. He will exult over you by singing a happy song.*

**Zephaniah 3:17 NLT**

*But God demonstrates His own love toward us, in that while we were still sinners, Christ died for us.*

**Romans 5:8 NKJV**

## A Timely Tip for Moms

Remember that God's love doesn't simply flow to your children . . . it flows to you, too. And because God loves you, you can be certain that you, like your child, are wonderfully made and amazingly blessed.

## Some Very Bright Ideas

Love has its source in God, for love is the very essence of His being.

**Kay Arthur**

Grin! God loves you! The rest of us will wonder what you've been up to.

**Anonymous**

Life in God is a great big hug that lasts forever!

**Barbara Johnson**

## A Mother-Daughter Prayer

*Dear Lord, the Bible teaches us that You are love. And, we know that You love us. We will accept Your love—and share it—now and always. Amen*

# The Best Excuse Is No Excuse

*Each of us will be rewarded for his own hard work.*

**1 Corinthians 3:8 TLB**

**W**hat is an excuse? Well, when you make up an excuse, that means that you try to come up with a good reason that you didn't do something that you should have done.

Anybody can make up excuses, and you can too. But you shouldn't get into the habit of making too many excuses. Why? Because excuses don't work. And why don't they work? Because everybody has already heard so many excuses that almost everybody can recognize excuses when they hear them.

So the next time you're tempted to make up an excuse, don't. Instead of making an excuse, do what you think is right. After all, the very best excuse of all . . . is no excuse.

## A Timely Tip for Girls

The habit of making excuses is a bad habit. Excuses lead to trouble. If you're in the habit of making excuses, the best day to stop that habit is today.

# More from God's Word

*It is God's will that your good lives should silence those who make foolish accusations against you. You are not slaves; you are free. But your freedom is not an excuse to do evil. You are free to live as God's slaves.*

**1 Peter 2:15-16 NLT**

*You can be sure that no immoral, impure, or greedy person will inherit the Kingdom of Christ and of God. For a greedy person is really an idolater who worships the things of this world. Don't be fooled by those who try to excuse these sins, for the terrible anger of God comes upon all those who disobey him.*

**Ephesians 5:5-6 NLT**

*Let us live in a right way . . . clothe yourselves with the Lord Jesus Christ and forget about satisfying your sinful self.*

**Romans 13:13-14 NCV**

# A Timely Tip for Moms

As a mom, you may hear lots and lots of excuses, some of which are valid, but many of which are not. It's your job to determine the difference between valid excuses and imaginary ones, and then to help your child understand the difference between the two.

## Some Very Bright Ideas

Making up a string of excuses is usually harder than doing the work.

**Marie T. Freeman**

Never use your problem as an excuse for bad attitudes or behavior.

**Joyce Meyer**

We need to stop focusing on our lacks and stop giving out excuses and start looking at and listening to Jesus.

**Anne Graham Lotz**

## A Mother-Daughter Prayer

*Dear Lord, when we are tempted to make excuses, help us to be strong as we accept responsibility for our actions. Amen*

# Obey God and Be Happy

*I will praise you, Lord, with all my heart. I will tell all the miracles you have done. I will be happy because of you; God Most High, I will sing praises to your name.*

**Psalm 9:1-2 NCV**

D o you want to be happy? Here are some things you should do: Love God and His Son, Jesus; obey the Golden Rule; and always try to do the right thing. When you do these things, you'll discover that happiness goes hand-in-hand with good behavior.

The happiest people do not misbehave; the happiest people are not cruel or greedy. The happiest people don't say unkind things. The happiest people are those who love God and follow His rules—starting with the Golden one.

## A Timely Tip for Girls

Even if you're a very good person, you shouldn't expect to be happy all the time. Sometimes, things will happen to make you sad, and it's okay to be sad when bad things happen to you or to your friends and family. But remember: through good times and bad, you'll always be happier if you obey the rules of your Father in heaven. So obey them!

## More from God's Word

*How happy are those whose way is blameless, who live according to the law of the Lord! Happy are those who keep His decrees and seek Him with all their heart.*

**Psalm 119:1-2 HCSB**

*Happy is the one whose help is the God of Jacob, whose hope is in the Lord his God.*

**Psalm 146:5 HCSB**

*How happy is everyone who fears the Lord, who walks in His ways!*

**Psalm 128:1 HCSB**

## A Timely Tip for Moms

Do you want to make your home life a continual feast? Learn to laugh and love, but not necessarily in that order.

## Some Very Bright Ideas

When we do what is right, we have contentment, peace, and happiness.

**Beverly LaHaye**

When we bring sunshine into the lives of others, we're warmed by it ourselves. When we spill a little happiness, it splashes on us.

**Barbara Johnson**

Smile—it increases your face value.

**Anonymous**

## A Mother-Daughter Prayer

*Dear Lord, You have given us more blessings than we can count. We will do our best to be joyful Christians as we give thanks for Your blessings, for Your love, and for Your Son. Amen*

# Think Before You Speak

*To everything there is a season...a time to keep silence, and a time to speak.*

**Ecclesiastes 3:1, 7 KJV**

Sometimes, it's easier to say the wrong thing than it is to say the right thing—especially if we're in a hurry to blurt out the first words that come into our heads. But, if we are patient and if we choose our words carefully, we can help other people feel better, and that's exactly what God wants us to do.

The Book of Proverbs tells us that the right words, spoken at the right time, can be wonderful gifts to our families and to our friends. That's why we should think about the things that we say before we say them, not after. When we do, our words make the world a better place, and that's exactly what God wants!

## A Timely Tip for Girls

If you can't think of something nice to say . . . don't say anything. Sometimes, the best use of a mouth is to keep it closed.

# More from God's Word

*Pleasant words are a honeycomb: sweet to the taste and health to the body.*

**Proverbs 16:24 HCSB**

*For the one who wants to love life and to see good days must keep his tongue from evil and his lips from speaking deceit.*

**1 Peter 3:10 HCSB**

*Avoid irreverent, empty speech, for this will produce an even greater measure of godlessness.*

**2 Timothy 2:16 HCSB**

# A Timely Tip for Moms

As a parent, it's up to you to establish the general tone of the conversations that occur in your home. Make certain that the tone you set is worthy of the One you worship.

## Some Very Bright Ideas

If you can't think of something nice to say, keep thinking.

**Criswell Freeman**

In all your deeds and words, you should look on Jesus as your model, whether you are keeping silence or speaking, whether you are alone or with others.

**St. Bonaventure**

Change the heart, and you change the speech.

**Warren Wiersbe**

## A Mother-Daughter Prayer

*Dear Lord, we know that You hear every word we say. Every day, we will try our best to say things that are honest, kind, and worthy of You. Amen*

# Your Amazing Talents!

*Now there are varieties of gifts, but the same Spirit. And there are varieties of ministries, and the same Lord.*

**1 Corinthians 12:4-5 NASB**

Face facts: you've got very special talents, talents that have been given to you by God. So here's a question: will you use your talents or not? God wants you to use your talents to become a better person and a better Christian. And that's what you should want for yourself.

As you're trying to figure out exactly what you're good at, be sure and talk about it with your parents. They can help you decide how best to use and improve the gifts God has given you.

## A Timely Tip for Girls

God gives you talents for a reason: to use them.

## More from God's Word

*Do not neglect the gift that is in you.*

**1 Timothy 4:14 HCSB**

*God has given gifts to each of you from his great variety of spiritual gifts. Manage them well so that God's generosity can flow through you.*

**1 Peter 4:10 NLT**

*Every good gift and every perfect gift is from above, and cometh down from the Father of lights.*

**James 1:17 KJV**

## A Timely Tip for Moms

Of course you want to help your child discover her hidden—or not so hidden—talents. A good place to start is by helping your child discover the topics and activities that are the most fun. Today's child's play may become tomorrow's passionate pursuit.

## Some Very Bright Ideas

God has given you special talents—now it's your turn to give them back to God.

**Marie T. Freeman**

You are a unique blend of talents, skills, and gifts, which makes you an indispensable member of the body of Christ.

**Charles Stanley**

You are the only person on earth who can use your ability.

**Zig Ziglar**

## A Mother-Daughter Prayer

*Lord, thank You for the talents You have given us. We will treasure those talents, and we will use them as we try our best to walk in the footsteps of Your Son. Amen*

# Draw a Picture Together about Your Talents

# Time for God

*I wait quietly before God, for my hope is in him.*

**Psalm 62:5 NLT**

**W**hen it comes to spending time with God, are you a "squeezer" or a "pleaser"? Do you squeeze God into your schedule with a prayer before mealtime, or do you please God by talking to Him far more often than that? If you're wise, you'll form the habit of spending time with God every day.

Even if you're the busiest girl on Planet Earth, you can still carve out a little time for God. And when you think about it, isn't that the very least you should do?

## A Timely Tip for Girls

The world is constantly vying for your attention, and sometimes the noise can be deafening. Remember the words of Elisabeth Elliot; she said, "The world is full of noise. Let us learn the art of silence, stillness, and solitude."

# More from God's Word

*Be still, and know that I am God.*

**Psalm 46:10 NKJV**

*But those who wait on the LORD shall renew their strength; they shall mount up with wings like eagles, they shall run and not be weary, they shall walk and not faint.*

**Isaiah 40:31 NKJV**

*Therefore humble yourselves under the mighty hand of God, that He may exalt you in due time.*

**1 Peter 5:6 NKJV**

## A Timely Tip for Moms

Finding time for God takes time . . . and it's up to you to find it. Try this: Begin each day with a few minutes of quiet time to organize your thoughts. During this time, read at least one uplifting Bible passage and thus begin your day on a positive, productive note.

## Some Very Bright Ideas

Finding time for God takes time . . . and it's up to you to find it.

**Criswell Freeman**

Frustration is not the will of God. There is time to do anything and everything that God wants us to do.

**Elisabeth Elliot**

The choices of time are binding in eternity.

**Jack MacArthur**

## A Mother-Daughter Prayer

*Lord, we will worship You every day. Help us discover the peace that can be ours when we welcome You into our hearts. Amen*

# Obeying God

*But be doers of the word and not hearers only.*

**James 1:22 HCSB**

How can you show God how much you love Him? By obeying His commandments, that's how! When you follow God's rules, you show Him that you have real respect for Him and for His Son.

Sometimes, you will be tempted to disobey God, but don't do it. And sometimes you'll be tempted to disobey your parents or your teachers . . . but don't do that, either.

When your parent steps away or a teacher looks away, it's up to you to control yourself. And of this you can be sure: If you really want to control yourself, you can do it!

## A Timely Tip for Girls

Associate with friends who, by their words and actions, encourage you to obey God.

## More from God's Word

*Therefore, get your minds ready for action, being self-disciplined, and set your hope completely on the grace to be brought to you at the revelation of Jesus Christ. As obedient children, do not be conformed to the desires of your former ignorance but, as the One who called you is holy, you also are to be holy in all your conduct.*

**1 Peter 1:13-15 HCSB**

*Who is wise and understanding among you? He should show his works by good conduct with wisdom's gentleness.*

**James 3:13 HCSB**

*You must follow the Lord your God and fear Him. You must keep His commands and listen to His voice; you must worship Him and remain faithful to Him.*

**Deuteronomy 13:4 HCSB**

## A Timely Tip for Moms

If your children don't learn obedience between the four walls of your home, they probably won't learn it anywhere else.

## Some Very Bright Ideas

Obedience invites Christ to show his incomparable strength in our mortal weakness.

**Beth Moore**

Every day, I find countless opportunities to decide whether I will obey God and demonstrate my love for Him or try to please myself or the world system. God is waiting for my choices.

**Bill Bright**

God does not want the forced obedience of slaves. Instead, He covets the voluntary love and obedience of children who love Him for Himself.

**Catherine Marshall**

## A Mother-Daughter Prayer

*Dear Lord, we want to be obedient Christians. Today and every day, help us understand Your rules and obey them. Amen*

# Be Thankful

*Our prayers for you are always spilling over into thanksgivings. We can't quit thanking God our Father and Jesus our Messiah for you!*

**Colossians 1:3 MSG**

Are you a thankful girl? You should be! Whether you realize it or not, you have much to be thankful for. And who has given you all the blessings you enjoy? Your parents are responsible, of course. But all of our blessings really start with God.

All of us should make thanksgiving a habit. Since we have been given so much, the least we can do is say "Thank You" to the One who has given us more blessings than we can possibly ever count.

## A Timely Tip for Girls

When is the best time to say "thanks" to God? Any time. God loves you all the time, and that's exactly why you should praise Him all the time.

# More from God's Word

*Give thanks to the Lord, for He is good; His faithful love endures forever.*

**Psalm 118:29 HCSB**

*I will give You thanks with all my heart.*

**Psalm 138:1 HCSB**

*And whatever you do, in word or in deed, do everything in the name of the Lord Jesus, giving thanks to God the Father through Him.*

**Colossians 3:17 HCSB**

# A Timely Tip for Moms

You are thankful to God for all His blessings, starting, of course, with your family. Make certain your children know how you feel.

## Some Very Bright Ideas

It is always possible to be thankful for what is given rather than to complain about what is not given. One or the other becomes a habit of life.

**Elisabeth Elliot**

One reason why we don't thank God for his answer to our prayer is that frequently we don't recognize them as being answers to our prayers. We just take his bountiful supply or dramatic action for granted when it comes.

**Evelyn Christenson**

Thanksgiving or complaining—these words express two contrastive attitudes of the souls of God's children in regard to His dealings with them. The soul that gives thanks can find comfort in everything; the soul that complains can find comfort in nothing.

**Hannah Whitall Smith**

## A Mother-Daughter Prayer

*Lord, You have plans for us that are bigger and better than we can imagine. We will trust You to take care of us, and we will try our best to obey Your rules, now and always. Amen*

# If You're Trying to Be Perfect

*The Lord says, "Forget what happened before, and do not think about the past. Look at the new thing I am going to do. It is already happening. Don't you see it? I will make a road in the desert and rivers in the dry land."*

**Isaiah 43:18-19 NCV**

If you're trying to be perfect, you're trying to do something that's impossible. No matter how much you try, you can't be a perfect person . . . and that's okay.

God doesn't expect you to live a mistake-free life—and neither should you. In the game of life, God expects you to try, but He doesn't always expect you to win. Sometimes, you'll make mistakes, but even then, you shouldn't give up!

So remember this: you don't have to be perfect to be a wonderful person. In fact, you don't even need to be "almost-perfect." You simply must try your best and leave the rest up to God.

## A Timely Tip for Girls

Don't be too hard on yourself: you don't have to be perfect to be wonderful.

## More from God's Word

*Those who wait for perfect weather will never plant seeds; those who look at every cloud will never harvest crops. Plant early in the morning, and work until evening, because you don't know if this or that will succeed. They might both do well.*

**Ecclesiastes 11:4, 6 NCV**

*Your beliefs about these things should be kept secret between you and God. People are happy if they can do what they think is right without feeling guilty.*

**Romans 14:22 NCV**

*The fear of human opinion disables; trusting in God protects you from that.*

**Proverbs 29:25 MSG**

## A Timely Tip for Moms

You, too, may be caught up in the modern-day push toward perfection, and if you are, your attitude will be contagious. When you "lighten up" on yourself, you will, in turn, do the same for your children.

## Some Very Bright Ideas

Because we are rooted and grounded in love, we can be relaxed and at ease, knowing that our acceptance is not based on our performance or our perfect behavior.

**Joyce Meyer**

A perfectionist resists the truth that growing up in Christ is a process.

**Susan Lenzkes**

Excellence is not perfection, but essentially a desire to be strong in the Lord and for the Lord.

**Cynthia Heald**

## A Mother-Daughter Prayer

*Dear Lord, help us remember that we don't have to be perfect. We will try hard to be good people, Lord, but we won't expect to be perfect people. Amen*

# Right and Wrong

*Lead a tranquil and quiet life in all godliness and dignity.*

**1 Timothy 2:2 HCSB**

If you're old enough to know right from wrong, then you're old enough to do something about it. In other words, you should always try to do the right thing, and you should also do your very best not to do the wrong thing.

The more self-control you have, the easier it is to do the right thing. Why? Because, when you learn to think first and do things next, you avoid lots of silly mistakes. So here's great advice: first, slow down long enough to figure out the right thing to do—and then do it. You'll make yourself happy, and you'll make lots of other people happy, too.

## A Timely Tip for Girls

Good behavior leads to a happy life. And bad behavior doesn't. Behave accordingly.

## More from God's Word

*As obedient children, do not be conformed to the desires of your former ignorance but, as the One who called you is holy, you also are to be holy in all your conduct.*

**1 Peter 1:14-15 HCSB**

*For this very reason, make every effort to supplement your faith with goodness, goodness with knowledge, knowledge with self-control, self-control with endurance, endurance with godliness.*

**2 Peter 1:5-6 HCSB**

*Therefore as you have received Christ Jesus the Lord, walk in Him.*

**Colossians 2:6 HCSB**

## A Timely Tip for Moms

When talking to your children about God, your actions speak much more loudly than your words. So behave accordingly.

## Some Very Bright Ideas

When your good behavior speaks for itself . . . don't interrupt.

**Anonymous**

Do nothing that you would not like to be doing when Jesus comes. Go no place where you would not like to be found when He returns.

**Corrie ten Boom**

There may be no trumpet sound or loud applause when we make a right decision, just a calm sense of resolution and peace.

**Gloria Gaither**

## A Mother-Daughter Prayer

*Dear Lord, there is a right way and a wrong way to live. Teach us the right way to live, Lord, this day and every day. Amen*

# Yes, Jesus Loves You

*Just as the Father has loved Me, I also have loved you. Remain in My love.*

**John 15:9 HCSB**

The Bible makes this promise: Jesus loves you. And how should that make you feel? Well, the fact that Jesus loves you should make you very happy indeed, so happy, in fact, that you try your best to do the things that Jesus wants you to do.

Jesus wants you to welcome Him into your heart, He wants you to love and obey God, and He wants you to be kind to people. These are all very good things to do . . . and the rest is up to you!

## A Timely Tip for Girls

Jesus loves you so much that He gave His life so that you might live forever with Him in heaven. And how can you repay Christ's love? By accepting Him into your heart and by obeying His rules. When you do, He will love you and bless you today, tomorrow, and forever.

## More from God's Word

*I am the good shepherd. The good shepherd lays down his life for the sheep.*

**John 10:11 NIV**

*Just as the Father has loved Me, I also have loved you. Remain in My love.*

**John 15:9 HCSB**

*Who will separate us from the love of Christ? Will tribulation, or distress, or persecution, or famine, or nakedness, or peril, or sword? But in all these things we overwhelmingly conquer through Him who loved us.*

**Romans 8:35, 37 NASB**

## A Timely Tip for Moms

Through His sacrifice on the cross, Jesus demonstrated His love for you and your child. As a responsible parent, it's up to you to make certain your youngster understands that Christ's love changes everything.

## Some Very Bright Ideas

Christ is with us . . . and the warmth is contagious.

**Joni Eareckson Tada**

The richest meaning of your life is contained in the idea that Christ loved you enough to give His life for you.

**Calvin Miller**

We need to start receiving love from the moment we are born and continue receiving it—and giving it out—until the day we die.

**Joyce Meyer**

## A Mother-Daughter Prayer

*Dear Jesus, we thank You for Your love, a love that never ends. We will return Your love, and we will share it with the world. Amen*

# Listen to Your Parents

*Listen carefully to wisdom; set your mind on understanding.*

**Proverbs 2:2 NCV**

Are you the kind of girl who listens carefully to the things your parents tell you? You should. Your parents want the very best for you. They want you to be happy and healthy; they want you to be smart and to do smart things. Your parents have much to teach you, and you have much to learn. So listen carefully to the things your mom and dad have to say. And ask lots of questions. When you do, you'll soon discover that your parents have lots of answers . . . lots of very good answers.

## A Timely Tip for Girls

Your parents love you and want to help you. Their job is to help . . . your job is to listen carefully to the things they say.

# More from God's Word

*Honor your father and your mother so that you may have a long life in the land that the Lord your God is giving you.*

**Exodus 20:12 HCSB**

*Listen, my son, to your father's instruction and do not forsake your mother's teaching.*

**Proverbs 1:8 NIV**

*Let them first learn to do their duty to their own family and to repay their parents or grandparents. That pleases God.*

**1 Timothy 5:4 NCV**

# A Timely Tip for Moms

If your child is uncommunicative, don't give up; continue to listen and keep responding with love and encouragement; in all likelihood, the communication between the two of you will eventually improve.

## Some Very Bright Ideas

Listening is loving.

**Zig Ziglar**

One of the best ways to encourage someone who's hurting is with your ears—by listening.

**Barbara Johnson**

The first duty of love is to listen.

**Paul Tillich**

The cliché is true: People don't care what we know until they know we care.

**Rick Warren**

## A Mother-Daughter Prayer

*Dear Lord, let us learn as much as we can as soon as we can, and let us be good examples for other people to follow. Amen*

# How Would He Behave?

*And he saith unto them, follow me, and I will make you fishers of men. And they straightway left their nets, and followed him.*

**Matthew 4:19-20 KJV**

If Jesus were here, how would He behave? He would be loving and forgiving. He would worship God with sincere devotion. He would serve other people, and He would always abide by the Golden Rule. If Jesus were here, He would stand up for truth and speak out against evil.

We read in the Bible that Jesus wants each of us to do our best to be like Him. We can't be perfect Christians, but we can do our best to obey God's commandments and to follow Christ's example. When we do so, we bring honor to the One who gave His life for each of us.

## A Timely Tip for Girls

When you have an important decision to make, stop for a minute and think about how Jesus would behave if He were in your shoes.

## More from God's Word

*Walk in a manner worthy of the God who calls you into His own kingdom and glory.*

**1 Thessalonians 2:12 NASB**

*And you shall do what is right and good in the sight of the Lord, that it may be well with you.*

**Deuteronomy 6:18 NKJV**

*I, therefore, the prisoner in the Lord, urge you to walk worthy of the calling you have received.*

**Ephesians 4:1 HCSB**

## A Timely Tip for Moms

Kids often imitate their parents, so act accordingly! The best way for your children to learn how to follow in Christ's footsteps is by following you while you follow Him!

## Some Very Bright Ideas

He leads us in the paths of righteousness wherever we are placed.

**Oswald Chambers**

The best evidence of our having the truth is our walking in the truth.

**Matthew Henry**

Life is a series of choices between the bad, the good, and the best. Everything depends on how we choose.

**Vance Havner**

## A Mother-Daughter Prayer

*Heavenly Father, we give thanks for our church and for the opportunity to worship there. Amen*

# A Pleasing Attitude

*Set your minds on what is above, not on what is on the earth.*

**Colossians 3:2 HCSB**

God knows everything about you, including your attitude. And when your attitude is good, God is pleased . . . very pleased.

Are you interested in pleasing God? Are you interested in pleasing your parents? Your teachers? And your friends? If so, try to make your attitude the best it can be. When you try hard to have a good attitude, you'll make other people feel better—and you'll make yourself feel better, too.

## A Timely Tip for Girls

Remember that you can choose to have a good attitude or a not-so good attitude. And it's a choice you make every day.

# More from God's Word

*For the word of God is living and powerful, and sharper than any two-edged sword, piercing even to the division of soul and spirit, and of joints and marrow, and is a discerner of the thoughts and intents of the heart.*

**Hebrews 4:12 NKJV**

*Make your own attitude that of Christ Jesus.*

**Philippians 2:5 HCSB**

*Don't work only while being watched, in order to please men, but as slaves of Christ, do God's will from your heart. Render service with a good attitude, as to the Lord and not to men.*

**Ephesians 6:6-7 HCSB**

# A Timely Tip for Moms

Parental attitudes are contagious. It's up to you to live your life—and treat your family—in a way that pleases God because He's watching carefully . . . and so, for that matter, are your kids.

## Some Very Bright Ideas

It never hurts your eyesight to look on the bright side of things.

**Barbara Johnson**

Some people complain that God put thorns on roses, while others praise Him for putting roses on thorns.

**Anonymous**

Never use your problem as an excuse for bad attitudes or behavior.

**Joyce Meyer**

## A Mother-Daughter Prayer

*Dear Lord, we pray for an attitude that pleases You. Even when we're angry, unhappy, tired, or upset, let us remember what it means to be good people and good Christians. Amen*

# Your Picture

*For God so loved the world that he gave his only Son, so that everyone who believes in him will not perish but have eternal life.*

**John 3:16 NLT**

If God had a refrigerator in heaven, your picture would be on it! And that fact should make you feel very good about the person you are and the person you can become.

God's love for you is bigger and more wonderful than you can imagine, So do this, and do it right now: accept God's love with open arms and welcome His Son Jesus into your heart. When you do, you'll feel better about yourself . . . and your life will be changed forever.

## A Timely Tip for Girls

Remember: God's love for you is too big to understand with your brain . . . but it's not too big to feel with your heart.

# More from God's Word

*For the LORD your God has arrived to live among you. He is a mighty savior. He will rejoice over you with great gladness. With his love, he will calm all your fears. He will exult over you by singing a happy song.*

**Zephaniah 3:17 NLT**

*But God demonstrates His own love toward us, in that while we were still sinners, Christ died for us.*

**Romans 5:8 NKJV**

*For he chose us in him before the creation of the world to be holy and blameless in his sight. In love he predestined us to be adopted as his sons through Jesus Christ, in accordance with his pleasure and will....*

**Ephesians 1:4-5 NIV**

## A Timely Tip for Moms

When you invite the love of God into your heart, everything changes . . . including you.

## Some Very Bright Ideas

Everything I possess of any worth is a direct product of God's love.

**Beth Moore**

He is the same yesterday, today, and forever, and His unchanging and unfailing love sustains me when nothing and no one else can.

**Bill Bright**

God proved his love on the cross.

**Billy Graham**

## A Mother-Daughter Prayer

*Dear Lord, we thank You for loving us. And we thank You for sending Your Son Jesus to this earth so that we can receive Your gift of eternal love and eternal life. We will praise You, Dear God, tonight, today, and forever. Amen*

# Your Most Important Book

*But grow in the grace and knowledge of our Lord and Savior Jesus Christ. To Him be the glory both now and forever. Amen.*

**2 Peter 3:18 NKJV**

What book contains everything that God has to say about His rules and His Son? The Bible, of course. If you read the Bible every day, you'll soon learn how God wants you to behave.

Since doing the right thing (and the smart thing) is important to God, it should be important to you, too. And you'll learn what's right by reading the Bible.

The Bible is the most important book you'll ever own. It's God's Holy Word. Read it every day, and follow its instructions. When you do, you'll be safe now and forever.

## A Timely Tip for Girls

Try to read your Bible with your parents every day. If they forget, remind them!

## More from God's Word

*There's nothing like the written Word of God for showing you the way to salvation through faith in Christ Jesus. Every part of Scripture is God-breathed and useful one way or another, showing us truth, exposing our rebellion, correcting our mistakes, training us to live God's way. Through the Word we are put together and shaped up for the tasks God has for us.*

**2 Timothy 3:15-17 MSG**

*For I am not ashamed of the gospel of Christ, for it is the power of God to salvation for everyone who believes.*

**Romans 1:16 NKJV**

*But the man who looks intently into the perfect law that gives freedom, and continues to do this, not forgetting what he has heard, but doing it—he will be blessed in what he does.*

**James 1:25 NIV**

## A Timely Tip for Moms

Be an example of self-control. When it comes to parenting, you can't really teach it if you won't really live it.

## Some Very Bright Ideas

Nobody ever outgrows Scripture; the book widens and deepens with our years.

**C. H. Spurgeon**

The Holy Scriptures are our letters from home.

**St. Augustine**

God will open up places of service for you as He sees you are ready. Meanwhile, study the Bible and give yourself a chance to grow.

**Warren Wiersbe**

## A Mother-Daughter Prayer

*Dear Lord, the Bible teaches us that it's good to be in control of our emotions and our actions. So help us slow down, Lord, so we can look before we leap and think before we act. Amen*

# How Much Is Too Much?

*Since we entered the world penniless and will leave it penniless, if we have bread on the table and shoes on our feet, that's enough.*

**1 Timothy 6:7-8 MSG**

Here's a question to think about tonight: How much stuff is too much stuff? Well, if your desire for stuff is getting in the way of your desire to know God, then you've got too much stuff—it's as simple as that.

If you find yourself worrying too much about stuff, it's time to change the way you think about the things you own. Stuff isn't really very important to God, and it shouldn't be too important to you.

## A Timely Tip for Girls

The world wants you to believe that "money and stuff" can buy happiness. Don't believe it! Genuine happiness comes not from money, but from the things that money can't buy—starting, of course, with your relationship to God and His only begotten Son.

## More from God's Word

*And He told them, "Watch out and be on guard against all greed, because one's life is not in the abundance of his possessions."*

**Luke 12:15 HCSB**

*He who trusts in his riches will fall, but the righteous will flourish . . . .*

**Proverbs 11:28 NKJV**

*No one can serve two masters. The person will hate one master and love the other, or will follow one master and refuse to follow the other. You cannot serve both God and worldly riches.*

**Matthew 6:24 NCV**

## A Timely Tip for Moms

Too much stuff doesn't ensure happiness. In fact, having too much stuff can actually prevent happiness.

## Some Very Bright Ideas

The more we stuff ourselves with material pleasures, the less we seem to appreciate life.

**Barbara Johnson**

Theirs is an endless road, a hopeless maze, who seek for goods before they seek for God.

**St. Bernard of Clairvaux**

Outside appearances, things like the clothes you wear or the car you drive, are important to other people but totally unimportant to God. Trust God.

**Marie T. Freeman**

## A Mother-Daughter Prayer

*Dear God, help us remember that the stuff we own isn't very important. What's really important is the love that we feel in our heart for our family, the love that we feel for Jesus, and the love that we feel for You. Amen*

# Slowing Down for God!

*Don't burn out; keep yourselves fueled and aflame. Be alert servants of the Master, cheerfully expectant. Don't quit in hard times; pray all the harder.*

**Romans 12:11-12 MSG**

Everybody knows you're a very busy girl. But here's a question: are you able to squeeze time into your schedule for God? Hopefully so!

Nothing is more important than the time you spend with your Heavenly Father. So take some time tonight and every night to pray and to thank God for His blessings. God will be glad you did, and you'll be glad, too.

## A Timely Tip for Girls

The world wants to grab every spare minute of your time, but God wants some of your time, too. When in doubt, trust God.

# More from God's Word

*You can't go wrong when you love others. When you add up everything in the law code, the sum total is love. But make sure that you don't get so absorbed and exhausted in taking care of all your day-by-day obligations that you lose track of the time and doze off, oblivious to God.*

**Romans 13:10-11 MSG**

*Jesus said, "You're tied down to the mundane; I'm in touch with what is beyond your horizons. You live in terms of what you see and touch. I'm living on other terms. I told you that you were missing God in all this. You're at a dead end. If you won't believe I am who I say I am, you're at the dead end of sins. You're missing God in your lives."*

**John 8:23-24 MSG**

# A Timely Tip for Moms

Do first things first, and keep your focus on high-priority tasks. And remember this: your highest priority should be your relationship with God and His Son.

## Some Very Bright Ideas

We often become mentally and spiritually worn out because we're so busy.

**Franklin Graham**

Frustration is not the will of God. There is time to do anything and everything that God wants us to do.

**Elisabeth Elliot**

Getting things accomplished isn't nearly as important as taking time for love.

**Janette Oke**

## A Mother-Daughter Prayer

*Dear Lord, we have lots to do every day, but nothing we do is more important than spending time with You. Help us remember to pray often and to read Your Bible every day. Amen*

# God's House

*For where two or three are gathered together in My name, I am there among them.*

**Matthew 18:20 HCSB**

When your parents take you to church, are you pleased to go? Hopefully so. After all, church is a wonderful place to learn about God's rules.

The church belongs to God just as surely as you belong to God. That's why the church is a good place to learn about God and about His Son Jesus.

So when your mom and dad take you to church, remember this: church is a fine place to be . . . and you're lucky to be there.

## A Timely Tip for Girls

Forget the excuses. If somebody starts making up reasons not to go to church, don't pay any attention . . . even if that person is you!

## More from God's Word

*And I also say to you that you are Peter, and on this rock I will build My church, and the forces of Hades will not overpower it. I will give you the keys of the kingdom of heaven, and whatever you bind on earth will have been bound in heaven, and whatever you loose on earth will have been loosed in heaven.*

**Matthew 16:18-19 HCSB**

*Now you are the body of Christ, and individual members of it.*

**1 Corinthians 12:27 HCSB**

*Be on guard for yourselves and for all the flock, among whom the Holy Spirit has appointed you as overseers, to shepherd the church of God, which He purchased with His own blood.*

**Acts 20:28 HCSB**

## A Timely Tip for Moms

Your attitude towards church will help determine your kid's attitude toward church . . . so celebrate accordingly!

## Some Very Bright Ideas

How beautiful it is to learn that grace isn't fragile, and that in the family of God we can fail and not be a failure.

**Gloria Gaither**

The church is where it's at. The first place of Christian service for any Christian is in a local church.

**Jerry Clower**

In God's economy you will be hard-pressed to find many examples of successful "Lone Rangers."

**Luci Swindoll**

## A Mother-Daughter Prayer

*Dear Lord, we thank You for Your church. When we are in church, we will learn about Your promises. And when we leave church, we will carry Your message into the world. Amen*

# Draw a Picture Together about Church

# Moving On

*Mockers can get a whole town agitated, but those who are wise will calm anger.*

**Proverbs 29:8 NLT**

**A**re you the kind of girl who is kind to everybody? Hopefully so!

Tomorrow, and every day after that, make sure that you're a person who is known for the kind way that you treat everybody. That's how God wants you to behave.

And if someone says something to you that isn't very nice, don't pay too much attention. Just forgive that person as quickly as you can, and try to move on . . . as quickly as you can.

## A Timely Tip for Girls

Be kind to everybody. Even when it's hard to be kind, it's worth it.

# More from God's Word

*Real wisdom, God's wisdom, begins with a holy life and is characterized by getting along with others. It is gentle and reasonable, overflowing with mercy and blessings, not hot one day and cold the next, not two-faced.*

**James 3:17 MSG**

*You have heard it said, "Love your neighbor and hate your enemy." But I tell you: Love your enemies and pray for those who persecute you, that you may be sons of your Father in heaven.*

**Matthew 5:43-45 NIV**

*Hatred stirs up trouble, but love forgives all wrongs.*

**Proverbs 10:12 NCV**

# A Timely Tip for Moms

Your children will learn how to treat others by watching you (not by listening to you!). Acts of kindness speak louder than words.

## Some Very Bright Ideas

As you're rushing through life, take time to stop a moment, look into people's eyes, say something kind, and try to make them laugh!

**Barbara Johnson**

Reach out and care for someone who needs the touch of hospitality. The time you spend caring today will be a love gift that will blossom into the fresh joy of God's Spirit in the future.

**Emilie Barnes**

A little kindly advice is better than a great deal of scolding.

**Fanny Crosby**

## A Mother-Daughter Prayer

*Dear Lord, sometimes people behave badly. When other people upset us, help us calm down quickly, and help us forgive them completely. Amen*

# Keep the Peace

*Love must be without hypocrisy. Detest evil; cling to what is good. Show family affection to one another with brotherly love. Outdo one another in showing honor.*

**Romans 12:9–10 HCSB**

Sometimes, it's easiest to become angry with the people we love the most. After all, we know that they'll still love us no matter how angry we become. But while it's easy to become angry at home, it's usually wrong.

The next time you're tempted to become angry with a brother, or a sister, or a parent, remember that these are the people who love you more than anybody else! Then, calm down. Because peace is always beautiful, especially when it's peace at your house.

## A Timely Tip for Girls

What if you're really having problems within your family? You've simply got to keep talking things over, even if it's hard. And, remember: what seems like a mountain today may turn out to be a molehill tomorrow.

# More from God's Word

*Their first responsibility is to show godliness at home and repay their parents by taking care of them. This is something that pleases God very much.*

**1 Timothy 5:4 NLT**

*Every kingdom divided against itself will be ruined, and every city or household divided against itself will not stand.*

**Matthew 12:25 NIV**

*You must choose for yourselves today whom you will serve . . . as for me and my family, we will serve the Lord.*

**Joshua 24:15 NCV**

# A Timely Tip for Moms

As the parent, it's up to you (not your child) to determine the focus of family life at your house. If you and your family members focus on God first, you're on the right track. If you're focused on other things first, it's time to step back and reorder your priorities.

## Some Very Bright Ideas

It matters that we should be true to one another, be loyal to what is a family—only a little family in the great Household, but still a family, with family love alive in it and action as a living bond.

**Amy Carmichael**

Money can build or buy a house. Add love to that, and you have a home. Add God to that, and you have a temple. You have "a little colony of the kingdom of heaven."

**Anne Ortlund**

I like to think of my family as a big, beautiful patchwork quilt—each of us so different yet stitched together by love and life experiences.

**Barbara Johnson**

## A Mother-Daughter Prayer

*Dear Lord, You have given us a priceless gift: our family. We praise You, Father, for our loved ones and for Your beloved Son Jesus. Amen*

# Forgiveness Can Be Hard

*Anyone who claims to live in God's light and hates a brother or sister is still in the dark.*

**1 John 2:9 MSG**

But God tells us that we must forgive other people, even when we'd rather not. So, if you're angry with anybody (or if you're upset by something you yourself have done) it's time to forgive. Right now!

But what if you have already tried to forgive somebody yet simply can't do it? Then you must keep trying. If you can't seem to forgive someone, you should keep asking God to help you until you do. And you can be sure of this: if you keep asking for God's help, He will give it.

## A Timely Tip for Girls

Because God has forgiven you, you can forgive yourself.

# More from God's Word

*See to it that no one repays evil for evil to anyone, but always pursue what is good for one another and for all.*

**1 Thessalonians 5:15 HCSB**

*A person's insight gives him patience, and his virtue is to overlook an offense.*

**Proverbs 19:11 HCSB**

*Be merciful, just as your Father also is merciful.*

**Luke 6:36 HCSB**

# A Timely Tip for Moms

Holding a grudge? Drop it! How can you expect your kids to forgive others if you don't? Never expect your children to be more forgiving than you are.

## Some Very Bright Ideas

If Jesus forgave those who nailed Him to the Cross, and if God forgives you and me, how can you withhold your forgiveness from someone else?

**Anne Graham Lotz**

An eye for an eye and a tooth for a tooth . . . and pretty soon, everybody's blind and wearing dentures.

**Anonymous**

As you forgive others, winter will soon make way for springtime as fresh joy pushes up through the soil of your heart.

**Barbara Johnson**

## A Mother-Daughter Prayer

*Dear Lord, sometimes it's very hard to forgive those who have hurt us, but with Your help, we can do it. Today, help us forgive others, just as You have already forgiven us. Amen*

# That Little Voice

*For God is pleased with you when, for the sake of your conscience, you patiently endure unfair treatment.*

**1 Peter 2:19 NLT**

When you know that you're doing what's right, you'll feel better about yourself. Why? Because you have a little voice in your head called your "conscience." Your conscience is a feeling that tells you whether something is right or wrong—and it's a feeling that makes you feel better about yourself when you know you've done the right thing.

Your conscience is an important tool. Pay attention to it! The more you listen to your conscience, the easier it is to behave yourself. So here's great advice: first, slow down long enough to figure out the right thing to do—and then do it! When you do, you'll be proud of yourself . . . and other people will be proud of you, too.

## A Timely Tip for Girls

That tiny little voice inside your head is called your conscience. Treat it like a trusted friend: Listen to the things it says; it's usually right!

# More from God's Word

*Now the goal of our instruction is love from a pure heart, a good conscience, and a sincere faith.*

**1 Timothy 1:5 HCSB**

*I always do my best to have a clear conscience toward God and men.*

**Acts 24:16 HCSB**

*Let us draw near with a true heart in full assurance of faith, our hearts sprinkled clean from an evil conscience and our bodies washed in pure water.*

**Hebrews 10:22 HCSB**

# A Timely Tip for Moms

Sometimes, the little voice that we hear in our heads can be the echoes of our own parents' voices . . . and now that we're parents ourselves, we're the ones whose words will echo down through the hearts and minds of future generations. It's a big responsibility, but with God's help, we're up to the challenge.

## Some Very Bright Ideas

God gave you a conscience for one reason—to use it.

**Criswell Freeman**

Your conscience is your alarm system. It's your protection.

**Charles Stanley**

It is neither safe nor prudent to do anything against one's conscience.

**Martin Luther**

## A Mother-Daughter Prayer

*Dear Lord, You have given us a conscience that tells us what is right and what is wrong. We will listen to that quiet voice, Father, so we can do the right thing today and every day. Amen*

# Telling the Truth

*Jesus answered, "I am the way and the truth and the life. No one comes to the Father except through me."*

**John 14:6 NIV**

Sometimes, telling the truth is hard, but even then, it's easier to tell the truth than it is to live with the consequences of telling a lie. You see, telling a lie can be easier in the beginning, but it's always harder in the end! In the end, when people find out that you've been untruthful, they may feel hurt and you will feel embarrassed.

So make this promise to yourself, and keep it: don't let lies rob you of your happiness. Instead, tell the truth from the start. You'll be doing yourself a big favor, and you'll be obeying the Word of God.

## A Timely Tip for Girls

When you tell the truth and live by God's Truth, you'll be very glad you did!

# More from God's Word

*You will know the truth, and the truth will set you free.*

**John 8:32 HCSB**

*"You are a king then?" Pilate asked. "You say that I'm a king,"
Jesus replied. "I was born for this, and I have come into the
world for this: to testify to the truth. Everyone who is of the truth
listens to My voice."*

**John 18:37 HCSB**

*For God's wrath is revealed from heaven against all godlessness
and unrighteousness of people who by their unrighteousness
suppress the truth.*

**Romans 1:18 HCSB**

## A Timely Tip for Moms

You know the importance of the Truth with a capital T.
Make sure that your kids know it, too.

## Some Very Bright Ideas

Those who walk in truth walk in liberty.

**Beth Moore**

The difficult truth about truth is that it often requires us to change our perspectives, attitudes, and rules for living.

**Susan Lenzkes**

Lying covers a multitude of sins—temporarily.

**D. L. Moody**

Truth will triumph. The Father of truth will win, and the followers of truth will be saved.

**Max Lucado**

## A Mother-Daughter Prayer

*Dear Lord, when telling the truth is hard, give us the courage to do what's right. Give us the courage to tell the truth. Amen*

# Everybody Makes Mistakes

*Instead, God has chosen the world's foolish things to shame the wise, and God has chosen the world's weak things to shame the strong.*

**1 Corinthians 1:27 HCSB**

Do you make mistakes? Of course you do . . . everybody does. When you make a mistake, you must try your best to learn from it so that you won't make the very same mistake again. And, if you have hurt someone—or if you have disobeyed God—you must ask for forgiveness.

Remember: mistakes are a part of life, but the biggest mistake you can make is to keep making the same mistake over and over and over again.

## A Timely Tip for Girls

If you make a mistake, the time to make things better is now, not later! The sooner you admit your mistake, the better.

## More from God's Word

*Therefore, if anyone is in Christ, he is a new creation; the old has gone, the new has come!*

**2 Corinthians 5:17 NIV**

*If we confess our sins to him, he is faithful and just to forgive us and to cleanse us from every wrong.*

**1 John 1:9 NLT**

*Have mercy on me, O God, according to your unfailing love; according to your great compassion blot out my transgressions. Wash away all my iniquity and cleanse me from my sin.*

**Psalm 51:1-2 NIV**

## A Timely Tip for Moms

It is not a sign of weakness when you apologize to your child. If you make a mistake, say so. When you do, your child will learn a valuable lesson.

## Some Very Bright Ideas

God is able to take mistakes, when they are committed to Him, and make of them something for our good and for His glory.

**Ruth Bell Graham**

Mature people are not emotionally and spiritually devastated by every mistake they make. They are able to maintain some kind of balance in their lives.

**Joyce Meyer**

We become a failure when we allow mistakes to take away our ability to learn, give, grow, and try again.

**Susan Lenzkes**

## A Mother-Daughter Prayer

*Dear Lord, everybody makes mistakes, including us. When we make mistakes, help us learn from them. Let us use our mistakes, Father, to become better people and better Christians. Amen*

# A Love That Lasts Forever

*I am the good shepherd. The good shepherd lays down his life for the sheep.*

**John 10:11 NIV**

You've probably heard the song "Jesus Loves Me." And exactly how much does He love you? He loves you so much that He gave His life so that you might live forever with Him in heaven.

How can you repay Christ's love? By accepting Him into your heart and by obeying His rules. When you do, He will love you and bless you today, tomorrow, and forever.

## A Timely Tip for Girls

Jesus loves me, this I know . . . but how much? Here's how much: Jesus loves you so much that He gave His life so that you might live forever with Him in heaven. And how can you repay Christ's love? By accepting Him into your heart and by obeying His rules. When you do, He will love you and bless you today, tomorrow, and forever.

## More from God's Word

*And I am convinced that nothing can ever separate us from his love. Whether we are high above the sky or in the deepest ocean, nothing in all creation will ever be able to separate us from the love of God that is revealed in Christ Jesus our Lord.*

**Romans 8:38–39 NLT**

*And remember, I am with you always, to the end of the age.*

**Matthew 28:20 HCSB**

*Just as the Father has loved Me, I also have loved you. Remain in My love.*

**John 15:9 HCSB**

## A Timely Tip for Moms

Jesus loves you. His love can—and should—be the cornerstone and the touchstone of your life.

## Some Very Bright Ideas

Jesus is all compassion. He never betrays us.

**Catherine Marshall**

We are never nearer Christ than when we find ourselves lost in a holy amazement at His unspeakable love.

**John Owen**

Love is an attribute of God. To love others is evidence of a genuine faith.

**Kay Arthur**

## A Mother-Daughter Prayer

*Dear Lord, we thank You for Your Son Jesus and for His love. Today, we will share His love with our family and friends. Amen*

# The Girl in the Mirror

*For you made us only a little lower than God, and you crowned us with glory and honor.*

**Psalm 8:5 NLT**

D o you really like the person you see when you look into the mirror? You should! After all, the person in the mirror is a very special person who is made—and loved—by God.

In fact, you are loved in many, many ways: God loves you, your parents love you, and your family loves you, for starters. So you should love yourself, too.

So here's something to think about: since God thinks you're special, and since so many people think you're special, isn't it about time for you to agree with them? Of course it is! It's time to say, "You're very wonderful and very special," to the person you see in the mirror.

## A Timely Tip for Girls

God loves you . . . and you should too.

# More from God's Word

*God began doing a good work in you, and I am sure he will continue it until it is finished when Jesus Christ comes again.*

**Philippians 1:6 NCV**

*For You formed my inward parts; You covered me in my mother's womb. I will praise You, for I am fearfully and wonderfully made; Marvelous are Your works.*

**Psalm 139:13-14 NKJV**

*You're blessed when you're content with just who you are—no more, no less. That's the moment you find yourselves proud owners of everything that can't be bought.*

**Matthew 5:5 MSG**

## A Timely Tip for Moms

If you want your daughter to admire the girl she sees in the mirror, then you should admire the woman you see in the mirror.

## Some Very Bright Ideas

Christianity is about acceptance, and if God accepts me as I am, then I had better do the same.

**Hugh Montefiore**

The great freedom Jesus gives us is to be ourselves, defined by His love and our inner qualities and gifts, rather than by any kind of show we put on for the world.

**Leslie Williams**

Don't wish to be anything but what you are, and try to be that perfectly.

**St. Francis of Sales**

## A Mother-Daughter Prayer

*Dear Lord, thank You for Your Son. Because Jesus loves us, we know that we are protected. Because Jesus loves us, we know that we have value. Because Jesus loves us, we know that our future is secure. Amen*

# The Time to Talk to God Is Now

*Then if my people who are called by my name will humble themselves and pray and seek my face and turn from their wicked ways, I will hear from heaven and will forgive their sins and heal their land.*

**2 Chronicles 7:14 NLT**

God promises that He hears your prayers—every one of them! So if you want to say something to God, you can start praying (with your eyes open or shut).

Whatever your need, no matter how great or small, pray about it and never lose hope. God is not just near; He is here, and He's ready to talk with you. Now!

## A Timely Tip for Girls

Sometimes, the answer to prayer is "No." God doesn't grant all of our requests, nor should He.

# More from God's Word

*And everything—whatever you ask in prayer, believing—you will receive.*

**Matthew 21:22 HCSB**

*Rejoice always! Pray constantly. Give thanks in everything, for this is God's will for you in Christ Jesus.*

**1 Thessalonians 5:16-18 HCSB**

*Therefore I want the men in every place to pray, lifting up holy hands without anger or argument.*

**1 Timothy 2:8 HCSB**

## A Timely Tip for Moms

God doesn't grant all of our requests, nor should He. We must help our children understand that our prayers are answered by a sovereign, all-knowing God, and that we must trust His answers.

## Some Very Bright Ideas

I have acted like I'm all alone, but the truth is that I never will be. When my prayers are weak, God is listening. When my words are rote, God is listening. When my heart is dry, amazingly God is still listening.

**Angela Thomas**

Prayer moves the arm that moves the world.

**Annie Armstrong**

Allow your dreams a place in your prayers and plans. God-given dreams can help you move into the future He is preparing for you.

**Barbara Johnson**

## A Mother-Daughter Prayer

*Dear Lord, thank You for hearing our prayers. We will pray often, and we will follow in the footsteps of your Son, this day and every day. Amen*

# Follow Jesus

*"Follow Me," Jesus told them, "and I will make you into fishers of men!" Immediately they left their nets and followed Him.*

**Mark 1:17-18 HCSB**

Who are you going to follow? Do yourself a favor—follow Jesus!

God's Word promises that when you follow in Christ's footsteps, you will learn how to behave yourself, and you'll learn how to live a good life. Jesus wants you to be a "new creation" through Him. And that's exactly what you should want for yourself, too. So talk with Jesus (through prayer) and walk with Him (by obeying His rules) now and forever.

## A Timely Tip for Girls

If you want to be a disciple of Christ . . . follow in His footsteps, obey His commandments, talk with Him often, tell others about Him, and share His never-ending love.

## More from God's Word

*Be imitators of God, therefore, as dearly loved children.*

**Ephesians 5:1 NIV**

*Work hard, but not just to please your masters when they are watching. As slaves of Christ, do the will of God with all your heart. Work with enthusiasm, as though you were working for the Lord rather than for people.*

**Ephesians 6:6-7 NLT**

*Then Jesus said to His disciples, "If anyone wants to come with Me, he must deny himself, take up his cross, and follow Me."*

**Matthew 16:24 HCSB**

## A Timely Tip for Moms

Jesus has invited you and your child to become His disciples. As a caring Christian parent, you must make sure that your youngster understands the importance of accepting His invitation.

## Some Very Bright Ideas

Jesus challenges you and me to keep our focus daily on the cross of His will if we want to be His disciples.

**Anne Graham Lotz**

How often it occurs to me, as it must to you, that it is far easier simply to cooperate with God!

**Beth Moore**

A disciple is a follower of Christ. That means you take on His priorities as your own. His agenda becomes your agenda. His mission becomes your mission.

**Charles Stanley**

## A Mother-Daughter Prayer

*Dear Lord, we want to follow Jesus this day and every day. Help us to become more like Him, and help us to share His message with our family and friends. Amen*

# God Solves Problems

*Since God assured us, "I'll never let you down, never walk off and leave you," we can boldly quote, God is there, ready to help; I'm fearless no matter what. Who or what can get to me?*

**Hebrews 13:5-6 MSG**

Do you have a problem that you haven't been able to solve? Welcome to the club! Life is full of problems that don't have easy solutions. But if you have a problem that you can't solve, there is something you can do: turn that problem over to God. He can handle it.

God has a way of solving our problems if we let Him; our job is to let Him. God can handle things that we can't. And the sooner we turn our concerns over to Him, the sooner He will go to work solving those troubles that are simply too big for us to handle.

If you're worried or discouraged, pray about it. Ask your parents and friends to pray about it, too. Then stop worrying because no problem is too big for God; not even yours.

## A Timely Tip for Girls

If you have a problem, remember that God is big enough and strong enough to handle any problem, including yours.

# More from God's Word

*Finally, my brethren, be strong in the Lord and in the power of His might. Put on the whole armor of God, that you may be able to stand against the wiles of the devil.*

**Ephesians 6:10-11 NKJV**

*The Lord your God in your midst, The Mighty One, will save; He will rejoice over you with gladness, He will quiet you with His love, He will rejoice over you with singing.*

**Zephaniah 3:17 NKJV**

*God is my shield, saving those whose hearts are true and right.*

**Psalm 7:10 NLT**

# A Timely Tip for Moms

Every family puts something or someone in first place. Does God occupy first place in your family? If so, congratulations! If not, it's time to reorder your priorities.

## Some Very Bright Ideas

He is always thinking about us. We are before his eyes. The Lord's eye never sleeps, but is always watching out for our welfare. We are continually on his heart.

**C. H. Spurgeon**

There is not a single thing that Jesus cannot change, control, and conquer because He is the living Lord.

**Franklin Graham**

God has power and He's willing to share it if we step out in faith and believe that He will.

**Bill Hybels**

## A Mother-Daughter Prayer

*Dear Lord, there's no problem that is too big for You. Thank You, Father, for protecting us today and forever. Amen*

# No Regrets

*Don't let your spirit rush to be angry, for anger abides in the heart of fools.*

**Ecclesiastes 7:9 HCSB**

**W**hen you're angry, you will be tempted to say things and do things that you'll be sorry about later. And, since you don't want to be sorry later, think before you do something! Instead of doing things in a hurry, slow down long enough to calm yourself down.

Jesus does not intend that you strike out against other people, and He doesn't intend that your heart be troubled by anger. Your heart should instead be filled with love, just like Jesus' heart was . . . and is!

## A Timely Tip for Girls

If you become angry, sometimes it's better to say less, not more. The best time to think about your words is before you speak them, not after.

## More from God's Word

*All bitterness, anger and wrath, insult and slander must be removed from you, along with all wickedness. And be kind and compassionate to one another, forgiving one another, just as God also forgave you in Christ.*

**Ephesians 4:31-32 HCSB**

*A gentle answer turns away anger, but a harsh word stirs up wrath.*

**Proverbs 15:1 HCSB**

*But now you must also put away all the following: anger, wrath, malice, slander, and filthy language from your mouth.*

**Colossians 3:8 HCSB**

## A Timely Tip for Moms

When your child becomes upset, you'll be tempted to become upset, too. Resist that temptation. Remember that in a house full of kids and grown-ups, you're the grown-up. And it's up to you to remain calm even when other, less mature members of the family can't.

## Some Very Bright Ideas

No one heals himself by wounding another.

**St. Ambrose**

Doomed are the hotheads! Unhappy are they who lose their cool and are too proud to say, "I'm sorry."

**Robert Schuller**

When you lose your temper . . . you lose.

**Criswell Freeman**

## A Mother-Daughter Prayer

*Dear Lord, when we become upset, calm us down. When we become angry, give us self-control. When we feel the urge to hurt other people, let us remember that Jesus forgave other folks, and we should, too. Amen*

# Who Controls You?

*Be imitators of God, therefore, as dearly loved children.*

**Ephesians 5:1 NIV**

Do you try hard to control yourself? If so, that's good because God wants all His children (including you) to behave themselves.

Sometimes, it's hard to be a well-behaved girl, especially if you have friends who don't behave nicely. But if your friends misbehave, don't imitate them. Instead, listen to your conscience, talk to your parents, and do the right thing . . . NOW!

## A Timely Tip for Girls

Start now! If you really want to become a well-behaved person, the best day to get started is this one.

# More from God's Word

*Whoever gives heed to instruction prospers, and blessed is he that trusts in the Lord.*

**Proverbs 16:20 NIV**

*For this very reason, make every effort to supplement your faith with goodness, goodness with knowledge, knowledge with self-control, self-control with endurance, endurance with godliness.*

**2 Peter 1:5-6 HCSB**

*He who heeds discipline shows the way to life, but whoever ignores correction leads others astray.*

**Proverbs 10:17 NIV**

# A Timely Tip for Moms

Be disciplined in your own approach to life. You can't teach it if you won't live it.

## Some Very Bright Ideas

Discipline is training that develops and corrects.

**Charles Stanley**

If I could just hang in there, being faithful to my own tasks, God would make me joyful and content. The responsibility is mine, but the power is His.

**Peg Rankin**

No horse gets anywhere until he is harnessed. No life ever grows great until it is focused, dedicated, disciplined.

**Harry Emerson Fosdick**

## A Mother-Daughter Prayer

*Dear Lord, the Bible teaches us to follow Jesus, and that's what we want to do. So, Father, please help us show other people what it means to be good people and good Christians. Amen*

# Listen to Your Conscience

*I always do my best to have a clear conscience toward God and men.*

**Acts 24:16 HCSB**

Your conscience is a little feeling that will usually tell you what to do and when to do it. Pay attention to that feeling, and trust it.

If you slow down and listen to your conscience, you'll usually stay out of trouble. And if you listen to your conscience, it won't be so hard to control your own behavior. Why? Because most of the time, your conscience already knows right from wrong. So don't be in such a hurry to do things. Instead of "jumping right in," listen to your conscience. In the end, you'll be very glad you did.

## A Timely Tip for Girls

If you're not sure what to do . . . slow down and listen to your conscience. That little voice inside your head is very dependable, but you can't depend upon it if you never listen to it. So stop, listen, and learn—your conscience is almost always right!

## More from God's Word

*Now the goal of our instruction is love from a pure heart, a good conscience, and a sincere faith.*

**1 Timothy 1:5 HCSB**

*If then you were raised with Christ, seek those things which are above, where Christ is, sitting at the right hand of God. Set your mind on things above, not on things on the earth.*

**Colossians 3:1-2 NKJV**

*And do not be conformed to this world, but be transformed by the renewing of your mind, that you may prove what is that good and acceptable and perfect will of God.*

**Romans 12:2 NKJV**

## A Timely Tip for Moms

Trust the quiet inner voice of your conscience: Treat your conscience as you would a trusted advisor.

## Some Very Bright Ideas

Do nothing that you would not like to be doing when Jesus comes. Go no place where you would not like to be found when He returns.

**Corrie ten Boom**

Don't be a half-Christian. There are too many of them in the world already. The world has a profound respect for a person who is sincere in his faith.

**Billy Graham**

Christians are the citizens of heaven, and while we are on earth, we ought to behave like heaven's citizens.

**Warren Wiersbe**

## A Mother-Daughter Prayer

*Dear Lord, in our hearts, we know right from wrong. Today, let us listen carefully to the conscience You have placed in our hearts. Amen*

# God's Greatest Promise

*I assure you: Anyone who believes has eternal life.*

**John 6:47 HCSB**

It's time to remind yourself of a promise that God made a long time ago—the promise that God sent His Son Jesus to save the world and to save you! And when you stop to think about it, there can be no greater promise than that.

No matter where you are, God is with you. God loves you, and He sent His Son so that you can live forever in heaven with your loved ones. WOW! That's the greatest promise in the history of the universe. The end.

## A Timely Tip for Girls

God's gift of eternal life is amazing. Talk to your mom about God's promise of eternal life, and what that promise means to you.

# More from God's Word

*I have written these things to you who believe in the name of the Son of God, so that you may know that you have eternal life.*

**1 John 5:13 HCSB**

*We do not want you to be uninformed, brothers, concerning those who are asleep, so that you will not grieve like the rest, who have no hope. Since we believe that Jesus died and rose again, in the same way God will bring with Him those who have fallen asleep through Jesus.*

**1 Thessalonians 4:13-14 HCSB**

*Jesus said to her, "I am the resurrection and the life. The one who believes in Me, even if he dies, will live. Everyone who lives and believes in Me will never die—ever. Do you believe this?"*

**John 11:25-26 HCSB**

# A Timely Tip for Moms

God offers a priceless gift: the gift of eternal life. Make certain that your youngster understands that the right moment to accept God's gift is always the present one.

## Some Very Bright Ideas

God loves you and wants you to experience peace and life—abundant and eternal.

**Billy Graham**

God has promised us abundance, peace, and eternal life. These treasures are ours for the asking; all we must do is claim them. One of the great mysteries of life is why on earth do so many of us wait so very long to lay claim to God's gifts?

**Marie T. Freeman**

The unfolding of our friendship with the Father will be a never-ending revelation stretching on into eternity.

**Catherine Marshall**

## A Mother-Daughter Prayer

*Dear Lord, Jesus died so that we can live forever with Him in heaven. Thank You, Father, for Your Son and for the priceless gift of eternal life. Amen*

# Jesus:
# the proof of God's love.

—

**Philip Yancey**

**Draw a Picture of You and Your Mom Having Fun**